TRULY GUIDED READING

Liz Simon

LAS *pedagogy and success*

Published in Australia by

LAS *pedagogy and success*
Adelaide. 5024. South Australia.

Email: information, orders Lizstempaddress@yahoo.com.au

Code: LAS 1
ISBN: 978-0-646-90781-9 (pbk)
ISBN: 978-0-9923909-5-2 (ebk)

© 2014 **LAS** *pedagogy and success*

First published January, 2014
Copyright © Liz Simon

National Library of Australia Cataloguing-in-Publication entry

Author:	Liz Simon
Title:	Truly Guided Reading/Elizabeth
ISBN:	ISBN: 978-0-646-90781-9 (pbk)

Subjects:	ReadIng study and teaching Primary.

Dewey Number: 372.414

Printed in Australia

To my dear early educator-mentor and friend, Monique Simon who set my pedagogical path and to my lovely daughter Justine Pepper who helped me, not only a preliminary edit of my book, but undertook the early formatting on her own volition.

Thank you.

What would writers do without excellent and perceptive editors? This honour goes to Marian Clift (educator) whose structural suggestions, especially, made my material so much easier to read.

Thank you.

Scott Zarcinas (DoctorZed Publishing www.doctorzed.com) is commended for helping me to publish both a hard copy and ebook. As well, he kindly 'brushed up' the graphic design of the book making it look more professional. A special delight were the doves accompanying the page numbers.

Thank you.

I want to also thank Marc Snelson (Flinders University) for his observation that I quote in 'Case Study #13' chapter 12, page 84. A big acknowledgement to Nathan Taylor and Marie Newcombe and the grade 3 children from West Beach Primary School for cooperating in the taking of the pictures for the front cover.

Contents

PREFACE

I will begin with information about the origins of Guided Reading forwarded to me by a New Zealand Reading Recovery tutor working in Westminster Borough, London during the 90's. I was also working in London at the time and she helped me 'put right' many misconceptions and incorrect teaching practices I had developed while trying to put Guided Reading into practice. My learning about Guided Reading did not stop there. In 'dribs and drabs' I learnt more about Guided Reading and with each piece of knowledge my Guided Reading became more effective and relaxed; more like focused conversations that Guided Reading should be.

I am forever indebted to this lovely lady.

Background information (*Shirley Bickler*)
Professor Dame Marie Clay carried out research in New Zealand Schools in the 1960's to observe closely what happened as new entrants to school learn to read and write. In collaboration with a group of teachers she explored a wide range of teaching procedures that might be effective with children experiencing reading difficulties. Marie Clay published a series of articles and educators such as Don Holdaway, Barbara Watson and many others took her ideas and began to devise techniques such as **Shared Reading**. *Practicing teachers around the country were looking closely at the reading process and began exploring the notion of* **Guided Reading**. *New Zealand teachers began to timetable a block most mornings to teach reading. This gradually evolved into a formal structure which was taken over as a model by the Teachers Colleges and to this day student teachers in New Zealand are taught techniques associated with Shared Reading and Guided Reading.*

Shared Reading – *whole class*
Guided Reading – *small reading groups*
Independent Activities – *small groups/individual*

These reading scenarios have become an integral part of the teaching to read, think and problem solve throughout schools in New Zealand: schools in U.S.A. (Balanced Literacy), Britain (National Literacy Strategy) and Australia, Victoria, South Australia, (Early Years Literacy Program).

When I was a Reading Recovery teacher I learned that it is far more effective if the correct teaching methods were put in place rather than adapting methods to suit me (not the child!). I admit that for a long time I was on the latter path rather than the former.

As a Literacy consultant I am now outside looking in and see and hear teachers voice misconceptions and apply misapplications. Education journal articles confirm many of my observations about what is done under the name 'Guided Reading.' I surmise that many teachers have been taking information from varied sources and have developed their own procedures or worse still have forsaken Guided Reading because they are confused and view it as not worth the effort that is involved. And there is effort, in the first months, associated with Guided Reading.

I am passionate about Guided Reading; it is a wonderful teaching practice that gives thinking strategies to children to become independent readers, readers for life. As students read and talk they internalize the thinking not only constructing literal meaning but thinking more deeply, for example, looking at a range of perspectives, 'what could be'.

INTRODUCTION

Misconceptions and Misapplications associated with Guided Reading.

Reading Recovery is the model. Like Reading Recovery Guided Reading is differentiated learning – you cater for varied learning needs, supporting delayed readers and further, inspiring more capable readers. It is a group activity, in the classroom, with a purpose or focus, therefore teachers are not inclined to react to errors; instead new learning builds on the known. Guided Reading ensures developmental, continuous and successful learning.

To make it clear from the beginning Guided Reading is **not**:

- Hearing children read. Listening to a child read, recording his reading behaviour and analysing his skill development has its place as an assessment tool but it is not instructional;

- 'Before Reading', drawing recounts of experiences or labelling, or listing, say, things the child would do with a friend. *(Note:* with a non-fiction book a short list is created, 'what is known' and 'questions' students would like answered (refer to chapter 12 page 78);

- 'During Reading' creating speech bubbles, finding and writing adjectives for example;

- 'After Reading' while in the Guided Reading group scenario, doing word studies, writing descriptions of characters and so on;

- A programme (it follows a structure but teachers respond to the needs of the reader);

- Reading a storybook in unison with the rest of the group;

- Listening while the teacher reads the book;

- Reading the story for the first time along with the teacher;

- Taking turns around the group to read a page/paragraph/sentence of a new story (except in the case of reading a play);

- A faltering limp through a too-difficult book;

- Reading for an audience;

- A time where the teacher is distracted when working with a group.

Guided Reading is:

Guided Reading **is** readers being supported (especially before reading); a private time when purposeful problem solving on unfamiliar text happens. It is an approach where texts are carefully chosen with a challenge or two to enable learning to take place e.g. an unfamiliar word where the teacher shows a problem solving strategy; shows how grammatical knowledge helps prediction. Guided Reading is independently reading, thinking and talking about texts. Guided Reading is children engaging in making meaning, predicting, confirming, connecting, searching, monitoring, questioning - questions that involve recall and clarification and questions that go beyond ... speculating about stories and content.

'What ultimately counts is the extent to which instruction requires students to think' (Alexander, 2010 citing Nystrand et al 1997); giving the students problem solving strategies to lead them to think their way to independent reading and critical judgements. The teacher's role is to guide the discourse so readers, in a social environment, internalize the process of asking themselves pertinent questions. Rather than comprehension being geared towards answering literal questions, students in Guided Reading share with each other their interpretations of what they have read. A teacher attending to the shared discussions will soon perceive whether a reader's understanding is occurring.

The central principle for a teacher of Guided Reading is that it blends **overt instruction** with **attentiveness**; a time for instructing and a time for listening.

To implement Guided Reading teachers:

- Group readers with the same/similar 'next' learning needs ('zone of proximal development', Vygotsky, 1978);

- Have reading material for early, developing readers that is levelled and carefully chosen;

- Have literature (novels and picture books) and more complex non-fiction for early fluent readers;

- Question and prompt in such a way that eventually children acquire and use self help strategies;

- Model the problem solving processes of reading for meaning, including questions children need to ask themselves;

- Encourage children to explore and exchange ideas and learn from each other when sharing responses to the text.

Guided Reading, if properly implemented, ensures that students read a new text successfully which helps them develop positive attitudes towards reading; gives students an opportunity to use the features of many different forms of texts. As well Guided Reading provides opportunities for students to develop and practise reading strategies necessary for reading independently and thoughtfully and allows teachers to closely observe the students in the group while they process unfamiliar texts.

The question is asked:

Do children really think about the content, ideas and issues as they read?

Thinking, comprehending is not an osmotic event (read and the child will comprehend). Students when comprehending think and apply different thinking strategies to bring understandings to their reading *before, during* and *after* reading. Not all students apply these strategies and need explicit instruction in making connections, predicting, inferring, questioning and so on. Children are taught how to think more deeply about ideas as they read. This happens not only during Guided Reading but other reading and writing scenarios in the classroom (e.g. Shared Reading, Text Deconstruction, Reading Aloud, Shared Writing, Oral).

It is also reasonable to forward the notion that children must be given texts that will allow them think as they read.

The first step is matching readers to texts they read with ease to maintain a sense of the meaning of the story or information. The reader is confronted with only one or two unfamiliar words in the text and the ideas and sentence structures are not too complex.

The next aspect is the teacher supporting the reader; orientating the reader to the story, stating clear, concise, immediate 'fix-up' or problem solving strategies as each child reads with the aim that the reader takes on these strategies themselves.

Most importantly, Guided Reading involves exploratory talk; talk that takes place between the children in the Guided Reading group and the teacher. Constructing interpretations of literature and issues are paramount. Group talk guided by the teacher helps readers internalize the thinking processes when they read alone.

During Guided Reading, children explore texts they would not be able to manage independently. They learn comprehension strategies such as visualizing settings, character actions, connecting their life experiences and knowledge to the reading, predicting what the story will be about, inferring a theme, determining the main points. Teachers model open ended questions and discussion behaviours that are appropriate to establish a supportive context for sharing and constructing interpretations of literature. These questions may lead children to,

- identify with the characters, evaluate the behaviour of characters and justify their views;

- offer different hypotheses;

- understandings of new vocabulary that assist inferential reading;

- confirm predictions;

- sequence retelling;

- want to seek answers, anticipate events and visualize events that are described;

- want to contribute constructively to shared discussion about literature, responding to and building on the views of others;

- offer differing perspectives;

- find how illustrations/visuals may highlight the text or have an influence on the text.

And there is much more.

As was stated earlier, exploratory talk is the mainstay of the interaction of the group. Children need to take on the talk for themselves during the introduction and discussion phases, forward their opinions, find textual evidence for those opinions and really listen to each other.

Exploratory talk is different from the Q (question) and A (answer) format, although that is probably where you will begin when first taking Guided Reading groups. But as you encourage children to share their interpretations, and attentively listen to each other you will find that rather than you asking question upon question, you will become more an observer or if you do respond to children's talk you will be non-committal, answering 'maybe', 'could be', 'perhaps', 'possibly' which moves them away from you, making them develop their own perspectives - making them feel that anything is possible and it is their responsibility to communicate the possibilities to the group. You encourage children to talk to each other and in so doing they learn to explore **their** ideas, reflect upon those ideas, clarify aspects they do not understand and challenge each other as readers.

Working with small groups, of course, provides the ideal opportunity for children to use exploratory talk to develop as active, meaning-seeking readers able to learn from each other. As a teacher you will see how this type of interaction has a marked effect on the growth of the mind of a reader.

*** 🕊 ***

There are many challenges facing teachers implementing Guided Reading. For example:

Having a clear set of beliefs and understandings about Guided Reading, in particular about the pedagogy associated with literacy learning and learning in general – the understandings a child has **now**, what a child can do now, and what we as teachers want the child to understand and do **next**. Knowing that instruction is all about children thinking; listening, giving information, with the asking of questions and commenting being the sources of reflection, leads the teacher into making decisions about:

- How I assess the attitudes, strengths and needs of students?

- How I group students/regroup students (if necessary);

- How I manage the rest of the class where they are non-disruptive; are involved in worthwhile tasks/assignments.

- How I select texts with appropriate challenges; that allow children to read most of the text successfully; that reinforce learning from the day before; that interest and motivate children; that reflect learning happening in the classroom (e.g. social studies topic);

- How I determine my objectives for the lesson;

- How I orientate children to the text – understanding the importance of behaviours such as *anticipation;*

- How I pace my lesson (there are time limits);

- When to stop the reading and initiate discussion (the session is evenly balanced);

- How to question, comment, prompt in such a way that it is diagnostic and eventually children acquire and use self-help strategies; generate their own questions and initiate discussions;

- How I evaluate the effectiveness of the session (e.g. observe and note children's ability to problem solve unfamiliar vocabulary, know the main point, spontaneously initiate discussion);

- How I implement Guided Reading sessions for older children who are reading and planning for research/assignment;

- When to begin Guided Reading (especially when to begin Guided Reading for first year at school children, the time of the year and what attitudes, knowledge and understandings need to be brought to Guided Reading by these learners.

It certainly assists if Guided Reading is a whole-school initiative; where a certain time in the day is set aside and leadership and extra-curricular staff are ready to support the classroom teacher.

Guided Reading has variations for different levels of readers and in this book will be referred to as **Early** Readers, **Developing** Readers and **Early Fluent** Readers.

1

> "Can't manage the class while I take small groups."
>
> "Receptions are particularly hard to manage."
>
> "Grades 3, 4, 5 fool around."
>
> "No worthwhile work done."

Chapter focal points
Independent Task Management
Whole class learning
Type of task

Focal point: Independent Task Management

There are ways that behaviour management can become a strong feature in every teacher's classroom during Guided Reading; behaviour that allows teachers to work uninterruptedly with small groups.

The independent tasks children do are interesting, worthwhile and importantly, <u>doable.</u>

Work sheets (black line masters or 'cheat sheets') may seem the easiest. The teacher may meticulously explain all aspects on the sheet - what the children need to do - but often the sheets are busy with many different tasks for the children to complete. For those children who are new to formalized learning or have some impediment that inhibits the listening or retaining of information they may know what the first task involves and after that the messages are forgotten. The result being that these children will not know what to do and will 'fool around' when they are supposed to be 'on task' during Independent Activities.
For early and developing readers manipulative, open ended tasks are highly recommended.

They take the form of, for example, a categorizing board and accompanying cards to place under the appropriate column on the board:

ly added to adjective forms make adverbs	
y	ly

happy
happily

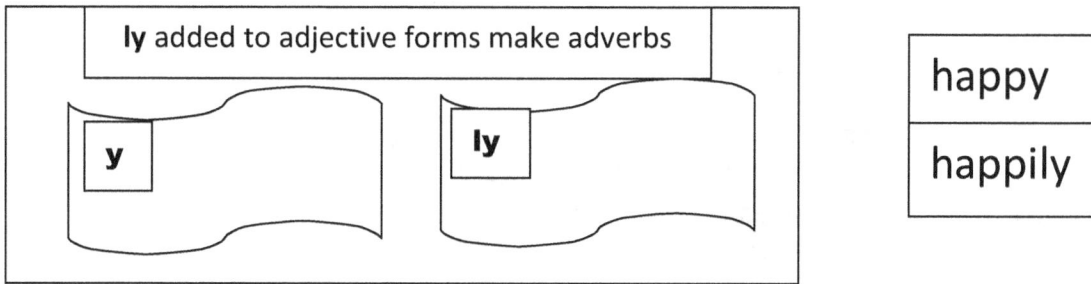

Children need to be well-versed in how to use or complete a task.

As you read further you will find that during Shared Reading (not Guided Reading) the class learns a concept for a week (it may be less time for more confident/older students) and on the last day they are shown and practise the activity that will go into a Learning Centre or something similar.

Being organized is a way a teacher overcomes behaviour difficulties.

Problems arise when children are kept waiting while the teacher is preparing materials, searching for books, pens etc. Labelling areas and items enable children to be more responsible for their collection of necessary items, but labelling is not enough. All materials must be complete, for example, all pencils sharpened, all the cards for a game to be in place (we all slip up at times, but not all the time!).

Before you begin Guided Reading be prepared.

Often teachers begin Guided Reading before they are prepared so refer to the below reminder list and mark 'what you have done/not done so far' (Figure 1).

Have you:	Yes	On the way	To do
Organized materials for easy access and return, for example, multiple copies of varied levels books, variety of genres easily accessible, independent tasks			
Prepared a box **(or similar)** for each group and in that box there are daily recording sheets, Running Record sheets, books to be read by the group next			
A class *Continuous Monitoring* graph ready to record progress			

Established a **'station'** where you will work with groups each day - boxes close at hand			
Established expectations **with** the children, that are relevant during Guided Reading e.g. *leave the teacher alone, pack away all materials, stay on task, finish your task before moving to next task, use a quiet voice, consult the task board*			
Read your rules every day for a week; revisit them when needed			
Place the rules where children can easily read and for you to remind			
Defined areas e.g. for reading big books, writing, high frequency word practise, audio books, computer			
Labelled **Learning tasks** and written simple instructions where appropriate			
Stored learning tasks where they are easily accessed by the children			
Colour coded activities to suit different group's learning needs			
Established an 'After Guided Reading high frequency word Learning Centre' for children levels 1-2 (may continue this activity to level 10)			
Prepared your **management task board** or something similar			
Prepared some generic learning centres to gradually introduce Independent Activity time to children e.g. poetry, big books, writing (general), games			
Grouped your children according to Running Record/comprehension knowledge			

Demonstrated every task/activity to the children prior use *(e.g. fishbowl)*			
Considered that children will work independently on well-planned and focused reading, writing, listening, and speaking tasks while you take small groups for Guided Reading			
In **week 1** of training children for Independent Activities, modelled how the children will read the task board, go to a learning centre, collect and use the activity and put the activity away (approx. 10 min session)			
In **week 2** of training children for Independent Activities, modelled how the children will move from one activity to the next (approx 15 min session)			
In **week 3** training, added a 3rd/4th movement (approximately 20 min session)			

Figure 1

Congratulations! Week 4, you could be ready to begin working with one Guided Reading group.

Helpful Hints
Begin independent activities and small group work slowly! Gradually introduce new learning Pre skill children in routines, tasks Gradually increase time Know your readers' levels

Behaviour Expectations during Guided Reading

In a fun way you guide children into creating appropriate expectations for Guided Reading. Introduce expectations as soon as possible, chart, read and role play every day, for at least four weeks.

Leave the teacher alone when she/he is working with small groups, individuals

Keep on task

Use a quiet voice

Consult the task board when you want to know what to do next (younger children use an activity at a time (approximately 3) stored in a basket kept on their desk)

Pack away all the materials you use before moving to the next activity

---

You do not have to have a lot of tasks!

Good management involves matching the task to the current learning happening in the classroom at that time.

Reading and re-reading always happens during independent activity time.

Early and developing readers re-read their books after Guided Reading. Early Fluent readers read independently, for example, they continue reading their novel or an information piece introduced to the group by the teacher. They may be reading for research, reading books by a particular author, reading and preparing questions for the next Guided Reading session, Reciprocal Teaching or Book Clubs (Book Clubs refer to Liz Simon's *Thinkers and Performers Bringing Critical Thinking Alive* (2010).

A management guide for children to refer to

Shifting responsibility to children during Independent Activity/Task time, allows you to work uninterrupted and able to concentrate fully on the small group. The expectation is that children will consult a **Task Board** (or something similar) to see what to do next rather than interrupting the teacher with "I've finished, what do I do next?"

TASK BOARD (Example)				
			Everyone practise spelling	
yellow	Guided Reading	Re-Read book from Guided Reading		News Plan
green	Rhymes and poems	Guided Reading	Continue reading novel	
orange	Bingo	Library	Guided Reading	Known Books
Red	Language games	Big Books	Word Centre	Hand-writing

Telling children what activity/where to go to the activity without referring to the Task Board can cause confusion. Always have children sitting in front of you before forming their groups. You read and check that they know where each activity is kept, not only the first activity but the following activities. This is done quickly so as not to take time away from Guided Reading.

Baskets with the activities contained within for each group, is generally favoured by teachers in the formative grades.

A **contract** with older students maybe the way to go.

Helpful Hints
◊ Tasks generally remain constant for a week.
◊ Current Tasks can be built upon; some tasks can be stored if not applicable for any group.
◊ Toileting can be solved by having all children's names attached to a poster with Velcro and they transfer their names to a clear plastic pocket, easily seen by the teacher.

> ◊ Games where there are 2-4 players are best placed as the first activity. When they work alone they complete tasks at their own pace. Some children may complete 3-4 tasks others may complete one.
>
> ◊ When the digital activities or audio books are not being easily accessed, immediately direct children to other tasks remembering that the focus **is** Guided Reading.

Focal Point: **Whole class learning**

Teachers being knowledgeable about where Independent Activities/Tasks come from?
Independent Activities/Tasks come from **whole class modelled learning**, literature (including non-fiction) studied during Shared Reading (e.g. big book), or a piece extracted from Read Aloud (placed on Interactive whiteboard or transparency placed on overhead projector) or from Shared Writing.

Each week: the whole class learn a particular concept (see: choosing a focus, figure 3). From the teaching/learning focus comes an Independent Activity or Activities/Tasks that relate(s) to the focus; activities that cater for varied learning needs and learning styles.

You are reinforcing learning done by the class. It is not a one-off; the activity is such that it is re-used. It integrates the learning needed for writing as well as reading.

Big books, short pieces extracted, say, from novels or articles or poetry have numerous text focuses and language focuses to choose from.

Figure 2 is an example of focuses from a fiction big book.

Rock and Roll Clyde (Magic Bean, 1996).
This story is about a boy in a wheelchair listening to all the physical antics his peers are able to do, but Clyde is not outdone as he competes in wheelchair races.
Language learning focuses in this piece include a number of models of: Question and answer structures Prepositions, adverbs Showing placement of capitals and lower case Sentence structure where the noun is followed by a pronoun Rhyming words Punctuation quotation marks, question and exclamation marks A spelling pattern - consonant, vowel and silent 'e' and initial consonant blends

Compound words
High frequency words

Comprehension:

The story allows readers to apply comprehension strategies e.g. prediction, making connections, inferring character traits, retelling, inferring alternative outcomes.

Figure 2

As you see there are any amount of focuses in *Rock and Roll Clyde*. Figure 3 will help you bring to mind a teaching /learning focus for the learning needs of your children.

Helpful Hint
During a staff meeting teachers could examine big books, for example, and list obvious Print, Text, Language and Word focuses on post-it notes and attach them to the front covers of each book.

Choosing any one of these Teaching/ learning focuses

PRINT
- ◊ Learning to scan pictures for meaningful information
- ◊ Locating print on the page
- ◊ Locating where to start reading
- ◊ Left-to-right directionality
- ◊ Reading left page before right
- ◊ Matching word-on-word
- ◊ First letter of a word

<u>TEXT</u> learning and teaching focuses

FICTION

Knowing the story (closed questions):
The parts of a story (title, characters, beginning, middle, ending) (Q. *How did it end*? (Q. *What happens after...(before*?)

Tell the facts that you have learned about...

Critical Analysis (open-ended questions):
The main idea

Problem, solution, possible causes and effects

Exploring themes (e.g. bullying, stereotyping, prejudice)

Analysis of the character (Q's. *How did you know what the character was like? Was the character described by the author? Was it the character's actions, motives that allowed interpretation of the character? Did the character's personality change during the story?*

Exploring the setting (Q. *Do the pictures tell the same story or do they go beyond the story?*)

Comparing differences/ sameness in stories

Inferring... *Because this was said/happened. This could mean...*

Taking different perspectives

Creative Thinking (generating possibilities):

How would you write the story?

Change the character to a different sex, or change the beginning, plot, ending, setting ... what difference does it make to the story?

How could you make the story more dramatic, interesting, humorous, scary?

Debate issues raised by the text content

Writing:

Organization and language structures of genres

<u>TEXT</u> learning and teaching focuses

NON-FICTION

Structures of non-fiction texts

How to read for information – how to access/ extract

Using the contents page/ glossary/ index

How to book-scan for research purposes

What are good questions to ask? (Q. *If you wanted to find out about _____ what book would you choose? When you scan, what key words would you look for?*)

Reading to answer pre-planned questions

Annotating

The language of non-fiction texts

LANGUAGE structures/features learning and teaching focuses

Identifying dialogue and its representation in print

Sentence beginnings relating to different genres (e.g. themes (topic sentences) noun groups. Time sequence (adverbs)

Varying verbs/using more explicit verbs, *shouted, whispered, lumbered*

Sentence structures – noun groups (words that add meaning to the noun e.g. articles, adjectives), adverbs and adverbial and prepositional phrases, different uses of final 's' (e.g. to denote plurals, possessive forms), abbreviations, singular, tense endings of regular verbs (e.g. look-ing, ed), irregular verbs (e.g. make, made), pronouns, she, he; her, his; they, their; noun/pronoun agreement, verb agreement, proper nouns, nominalization

Comparing simple, compound, complex sentences

Language that creates moods (e.g. sympathy/antipathy), imagery, effects emotions, perceptions, causes tension

Exploring colloquial phrases, idioms

Becoming familiar with literary features (e.g. alliteration, onomatopoeia)

Key words within sentences

Punctuation, paragraphing (why paragraphing?), differences between phrases, sentences, clauses, sub-clauses

---

WORD learning and teaching focuses

High-frequency words, root words(e .g. move/remove/removed), prefixes(opposite meanings e.g. un) and suffixes (change grammatical forms e.g. ed), digraphs (e.g. ay, ai, sh)

Consonant blends (e.g. bl), compound words, contractions (e.g. do not/ don't), silent letters, phonemes (same sounds, different letters), long vowels, homonyms (e.g. same spelling different meaning), acronyms

Working with synonyms /antonyms

Demonstrating the use of problem solving strategies, for example,
- dividing words into syllables
- searching for visual patterns e.g. ough

Etymologies

Abbreviations

Developing dictionary skills

Figure 3

Planning whole class focused learning

A Shared Reading (or deconstructing text) weekly plan may look something like the example plan (figure 4, below). There is an emphasis on meaning (day 1), the focus of learning (the concept) is highlighted on days 2, 3, 4 and examined in different ways each one of those days. By the 5th day the teacher has prepared an activity for a particular group or 3-4 tired activities (see *Type of Task*, below) to be demonstrated and then placed in the appropriate Learning Centre.

Figure 4 is an example of planned Shared Reading - non-fiction text:

Big Book: *Life of a duck (non-fiction)*
Learning Focus: *contents page/page numbers/headings (efficient way of finding information)*
Day 1: *Introduction, list questions children ask, will they be answered in this book? – look at contents; Why do books list contents (groups of 4 discuss and write a reason on a post – it note)*
Each day ask recall questions about previous day's learning
Day 2: *Read contents – 'Hatching' child finds the page it is on, 3 more children choosing contents and finding the pages. Refer to questions asked. From information in contents can their questions be answered? Read the chapter to confirm the answer.*
Day 3: *groups look at other non-fiction books and list different ways contents are presented. Read the chapter to confirm the answer.*
Day 4: *groups look at fiction books and list different ways contents are presented. Look at questions asked, read the chapter in 'Life of a duck' to confirm the answer.*
Day 5: *Pairs begin to make their own contents page about ducks (future books to be made).*

Figure 4

Focal point: **Type of Task**

When deciding on the independent task bear in mind whether you are reinforcing learning, extending students' skills and thinking and whether students of all abilities will be successful with the task you design. You can extend the consolidation of the concept by purchasing commercial material and include them in the appropriate learning centres.

Children are given worthwhile, purposeful reading and writing activities. Reinforcing tasks are mainly manipulative or open ended activity or generic task cards or sheets. Each child is given an appropriate reinforcement <u>or</u> is appropriately challenged.

A manipulative activity for particular groups

Examples of manipulative tasks are (a) 'correct punctuation mark insertion' activity, (b) categorizing adjectives, or (c) manipulating figures.

Colour code so the students in that group know to access it.

(a)

Place the punctuation mark that goes with the statement. Place the punctuation mark that goes with the question.	
"Can you kick a ball above the wall	or jump so high that you almost fly"
"No, but I can ride",	said Clyde

?
.

(b)

Adjectives There are different kinds of adjectives			
factual describer	evaluative describer	quantifier	classifier
brown	fearful row		Science lesson

slushy
undersized

(c)

Move the figures and tell a story.

Open-ended task

An example of an open ended task would be writing in literacy journals something that the children have recently learnt.

Two or three tiered activities

Each task card is colour coded to suit each group. You can focus all of the students on the same essential understandings or skills but at different levels of complexity, abstractedness and open-endedness. A three-tiered example is below. The focus of learning being: Recount a story. (See Black line masters 13, 14, pages 117, 118, for a variety of 3-tired activities).

Write how the story began and ended.	Write a recount of all the parts of the story – beginning, middle, ending.	Change the beginning and ending of the story.
R	B	Y

Generic comprehension sheet

Children become familiar with generic comprehension sheets and therefore they do not need long explanations. The sheets are in a simple form and yet are effective for reinforcing various literacy learning concepts. For examples, see Black line masters 7-12, pages 111 – 116, for a variety generic comprehension sheets.

RECOUNTING THE STORY
Name:
Date:
Title

Characters:
Beginning:
Middle:

Example of storage for easy access to activities

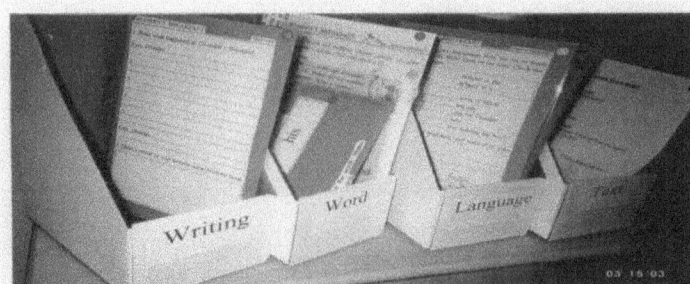

Ongoing tasks for early fluent readers

Fluent readers work independently or in small groups on, for example:

- Book reviews. These have a genuine place in the classroom as they are found in newspapers and magazines (the world outside school).

- Record recent literacy learning in 'Literacy Learning Journals' (cover, Black line master 16, page 120) for example, questions for discussion, interesting literacy items learnt, aspects that children may need to reflect on, what they learned about an author's treatment of the main character and so on.

- Continue reading text introduced in Guided Reading: completing graphic organizers (e.g. mind map), preparing questions for group discussion.

- Work on insert the themed or Inquiry writing connected to content area.

Use online chat forums such as blogs. These capabilities allow communication between students (and teachers, parents). A user can post a comment about books just read and students in the group can post responses. Chat mediums enhance engagement and enjoyment of texts, whether fiction or information texts read in Guided Reading. A great benefit is that children can, also, post their comments from home.

2

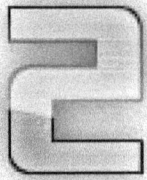

Chapter focal points

Challenging the use of black line masters that accompany small books

Scheduling daily Guided Reading

Focal point: Challenging the use of black line masters that accompany small books

In Chapter 1 it was laid out that independent tasks develop from whole class teaching and learning - Shared Reading, Text Deconstruction, Read Aloud or Shared Writing (joint construction). A concept is focused on each day for a week (less time for more advanced students).

You could give the children a black line master that is specific to the book just read in Guided Reading, but it takes time to explain, time that could be more productively used during Guided Reading, for example, another Guided Reading group could be worked with or more time could be spent discussing the 'just read' book with the group.

Published teacher resource books that accompany small books obstruct a teacher's judgement; the 'then and there' response that is needed for the particular problem that has arisen, for example, a child comes to an unfamiliar word and the teacher reminds him of the strategy, *Think about the story and think what the word could be*. Teachers judge the nature of the response whether it is a verbal modelling of a thinking strategy or moving the responsibility to the child, *What can you do to help yourself*.

Focal point: Scheduling Guided Reading

If the statement had been, '... once a week for a group' I could agree on the proviso that this group are fluent readers and their understandings are obvious.

However, I do not think that classes are homogeneous, just the opposite, classes are more likely to have readers at various points on a reading continuum. Guided Reading (or Reciprocal Teaching or Book Clubs) **should happen every day in a classroom**.

Small group reading happens for about 45 minutes each day. In the early years, three groups a session should be the norm. Groups who are reading longer text most likely it will be 2 groups a session in the 45 minute period.

Groups experience Guided Reading for different amounts of time a week – a low level group would meet with the teacher 4 days a week, a moderate level group 3 days a week, a more advanced group 2 days week, and a brilliant group 1 day a week.

A *weekly schedule* for early, developing and early fluent readers could look something like the below:

Monday	Tuesday	Wednesday	Thursday	Friday
Red	Red	Red	Red	Green
Green	Green	Orange	Orange	Orange
Blue	Yellow	Yellow	Yellow	Blue

A *weekly schedule* for older readers would look something like this:

Monday	Tuesday	Wednesday	Thursday	Friday
Book Club (orientation)	Red	Red	Book Club (discussion)	Red
Green	Book Club (orientation)	Reciprocal Teaching	Green	Book Club (discussion)

Of course, these schedules are the ideal. Large class numbers can make teachers feel they are not doing justice to their readers; not taking them enough times in Guided Reading.

Reader numbers for groups

Readers to Levels 1-9 read aloud, so 4-5 children at these developmental levels are sufficient.

Reception year teachers take the first group of level 1 readers for Guided Reading when they have ample alphabet knowledge (approximately 75%), (see chapter 11, page 75). They give these children a really good start. Then as more children are ready to begin Guided Reading, the first group will be seen fewer times.

Readers Level 10 onwards read silently and the group can be larger, 6-8 children.

3

> *Guided Reading inevitably turns into word study.*
>
> *The teacher reacts to the 'ent' words in the text; this study occupies most of the Guided Reading time.*

Chapter focal points
Students learn reading strategies 'at the point of need'   Decoding strategies termed as 'Fix-up strategies' and thinking strategies termed as 'Comprehension strategies'   Comprehension strategies defined   Comprehension strategies – example questions to model   How these comprehension strategies fit into a Guided Reading lesson?

Focal point: **Students learn reading strategies 'at the point of need'**

Guided Reading is **not** the time to study words. Writing (spelling) is the time to study words. Guided Reading is the time when 'Fix-up' (figure 5, page 26-27) and comprehension strategies (page 27-33) are taught <u>at the point of need</u>.

The established principles of the teaching aims of Guided Reading are:

- ✓ Giving children strategies and practise to read independently; there is an interplay between semantic, syntactic, and visual as they read;

- ✓ Inculcating thinking processes so children comprehend the literal and beyond;

- ✓ Encouraging children to read, think and talk their way to constructing meaning;

- ✓ Children, when reading, will become users of 'Fix-up' strategies (*how can you help yourself?*) and thinking strategies (comprehension strategies).

Before reading:

Importantly, know your readers and before they read foreshadow difficulties any child may have with particular vocabulary when reading independently. A further aspect is to limit the introduction of new words, remembering there should only be one or two challenges (unfamiliar words) for the reader, anyhow.

During reading:

If readers pause during reading because a new or unknown word is perplexing, you quickly tell a 'Fix-up' strategy (figure 5) or alternatively tell the word.

After reading

Choose one word only to reinforce a strategy. For example, begin by bringing to the reader's attention a 'Fix-up' strategy you modelled during reading, 'how the word links to a known word', *You remember how the character reacted at the beginning and the word used was 'scared', this word means the same; it begins with /fr/ so what could it be*?

You could then use the words to begin the discussion, *Why do you think the author wrote words like, scared, frightened*?

Vocabulary is extended this way during Guided Reading; an extensive vocabulary assists reading proficiency, both fluency and understanding.

Focal points: **Decoding strategies termed as 'Fix-up strategies' and thinking strategies termed as 'Comprehension strategies'**

FIX–UP Strategies children take on themselves to become independent readers.

FIX-UP STRATEGIES
Children handle their own books, turn the pages. The aim is for the children to eventually ask themselves these questions; use these **fix-up** strategies.
Remember what the story is about. What word do you think it could be?
Read that part again and see if you can find out what that word is.
Does that make sense/sound right? Does that look right?
Listen to yourself read … think about the story

What letter does the word begin with? (and when secure) *end with?*

Say the word slowly, what is the first/next/last sound you can hear?

Put the child's finger over part of the word to reveal the blend ... sn ⬭ *What do the 2/3 letters together sound like?*

What is the sound on the end? (referring to ing, ed, er, s, es)

What can you see in the middle of the word?

What is the small word you can see in this word?

Which word could it be ... went or jump?

Moving to, How can you help yourself?

Strategies the children are learning:

- o Monitoring themselves when they read, searching for information, cross-checking (using meaning as well as confirming visual);

- o Knowing the story, they can predict words;

- o **Confirming** their predictions by knowing that the story must make sense and sound right and look right;

- o Synthesizing strategy use.

Figure 5

Learning ten comprehension thinking strategies

As stated at the beginning of this chapter the aim of Guided Reading is to give children strategies and practise so they read independently. At the same time, they develop thinking processes so they comprehend, analyse, make judgements and come to conclusions.

Some children have a single-minded approach, where their attention is fully on decoding and this causes them to lose track of meaning as they read 'they perceive reading as a mechanical task rather than an interactive, meaning-based process' (Concannon-Gibney & Murphy, 2010 citing Rosenblatt, 1994). I think many teachers would relate to this comment made about developing readers ... "They struggle to comprehend...they'd sound it out, they didn't expect it to make sense" (Concannon-Gibney & Murphy, 2010).

Children will enjoy and be enthusiastic readers if they explore the story or information. Give them a repertoire of comprehension thinking strategies as well as 'Fix-up' thinking strategies (the ten + one, ten comprehension strategies + 'Fix-up' strategies).

You could focus on explicitly learning a comprehension thinking strategy over a period of time during Shared Reading or Read Aloud. For example, you could spend two weeks to a month exclusively concentrating on inferring, what it means to infer, how authors allow the reader to infer and how inferring assists reading.

Reinforce this knowledge as you guide children in internalizing comprehension strategies during Guided Reading.

Focal point: **Comprehension strategies defined**

Whether modelling happens during Shared Reading, Read Aloud or Guided Reading it is short, the teacher is knowledgeable and his language is precise; he verbalizes how a skilful strategic reader **actively makes meaning** by:

MAKING CONNECTIONS

When teachers introduce topics/concepts about which their students know little, they need to build bridges, use the familiar to help students discover the unknown. Active recalling of what they know can help students make sense/remember what they read.

The 'comprehension track' begins when we activate prior knowledge and experience (schema, or background knowledge) that children bring to reading and connect or reinforce the new material they are reading. It not only gives reading a purpose but the more children **anticipate** ideas, grammatical patterns and vocabulary the more impact it has when children read and affirm their anticipations.

It is important to link prior knowledge of how the story/information relates to their lives. 'By activating relevant prior knowledge before reading, readers develop expectations and questions that give them the momentum to read in a more focused way. The level of difficulty of a book varies depending upon a child's prior experience and what he or she brings to the text' (Ellin Keene and Susan Zimmerman, 1997). Catch phrases associated with making connections, are '*connecting text to self, connecting text to text, connecting text to the world*'.

PREDICTING

Having prior knowledge and experiences, children predict - they foretell and their literal prediction is proven by evidence in the text. Teachers begin by asking the group, *Looking at the cover picture and the title, what do you think this story is about*? Or as children are reading, *Knowing the story, what do you think that word could be?*

As readers become more confident, teachers tell children to *Read the title, look at the cover information, read the blurb (information about the story, generally on the back cover), read the contents and first page or two, and predict what the story/information could be about.* You may also ask them to look at pictures and diagrams.

VISUALIZING

Proficient readers **evoke sensory images;** they create visual and other sensory images to make sense of what they read; to deepen their understanding of the text. Active, visual verbs and specific nouns and noun groups, adverbial and prepositional phrases especially 'paint' pictures in reader's minds, for example, visualizing a descriptive setting helps readers know what and why the plot is constructed the way it is.

Read a story in Read Aloud and cover certain pictures, ask the class to form pictures in their heads of, say, an object, the setting and the problem. For example, children visualize the character from what is written about his actions. They **infer** how he may be dressed, what his appearance may be, what his movements may be, what his character traits are. Then ask the children to Think, Pair, Share (*you ask a question or make a comment, the children think for a moment, turn to each other and share their thinking*) and compare their 'mind pictures' with a partner. Poetry is a great medium with its images and similes and metaphors that give ample opportunities for varied interpretations.

Children can visualize and predict progressing events. They can visualize changes happening e.g. behavioural changes and this helps them understand causes associated with the change.

Children making comparisons when reading non-fiction material can be directed to visualize sizes, lengths, distance, time and maybe the weight of a baby elephant!

Visualizing is closely connected to inferring.

INFERRING

The definition of inferring is readers drawing logical conclusions and educated guesses, and using the information to make generalizations. A reader takes what they already know and merges it with clues in the text to make judgments and responses e.g. offer opinions, solutions, all the time never knowing if the inference is what the author meant.

An author does not always tell everything. A proficient reader thinks ahead in a story, inferring, anticipating events, drawing conclusions; he or she has the ability to use context to deduce meanings (including unfamiliar words) and interpret ideas. In discussion they persuade readers to their point of view and give logical reasons why they think as they do.

Making an inference involves several strategies working together – questioning the text, connecting the text to what is known, readers filling in the gaps by visualizing what could be. Readers interpret, for example, themes in stories, big ideas in information. When readers infer they delve deeper into the essence of texts often bringing their own unique interpretations to the text. Inferring is often called, 'Reading between the lines.'

When teaching 'inferring', children need to know the difference between **inferring** (their reasonable assumption most likely will not be proven) and **predicting** (the answer is in the text).

Then: Before, during and after reading you ask a question that prompts inferences to be made e.g. *Why do you think the author called the story...?*

Follow up questions are asked, *What have you inferred from reading...? Why do you say that...? What is in the text that leads you to that conclusion? Whose point of view do you think the article mostly pays attention to?*

When making an inference children justify their idea by giving a relevant example from the text that sparked their inference, *Explain... Why do you think that?*

ISOLATING MAIN POINTS/IDEAS (THEMES, KEY WORDS)

When activating prior knowledge children isolate the essential idea in the whole piece of fiction or non-fiction reading; non-fiction they, also, take the essential idea of each paragraph. Textual clues and features and structures in fiction and non-fiction also signal importance.

This sounds easy. But for many students it is not (especially when reading non-fiction) and lots of modelling in front of the children needs to take place.

When explicitly teaching 'main points' show children how to use cues to extract salient information, for example, the **theme (noun group)** written at the beginning of each paragraph and **key words** written throughout.

The more children know about a task, the content, the text features and structures the easier it is for them to anticipate what is to come and confirm important ideas while reading. Follow-up what has been learned with specially designed tasks, for example:
In groups of two, read a short piece of information and the pairs discuss and decide which are:

Main points	Interesting points

When reading fiction they read knowing the main points to focus on are:

- story theme;

- main characters;

- beginning;

- ending;

- cause;

- problem;

- effect, solution (see chart on page 102).

When reading non-fiction they read for specific information; they know the purpose (e.g. question) and this determines what to pay close attention to and what to ignore. More specifically as they read they notice:

- title, headings and subheadings, framed text, captions;

- the themes, topic sentences (generally the beginning sentence of paragraphs);

- key words and phrases (not entire sentences); words italicised or in bold print, fonts and effects, illustrations/ photographs, comparison drawings, graphics, diagrams, close ups, cutaways, maps, charts, tables, graphs, text organizers (index, preface, table of contents, glossary and appendix).   (See chart on page 102).

Proficient readers make decisions about the most important ideas and themes in a text and use these decisions to focus their attention as they read.

SUMMARIZING

Summarizing is closely associated with 'Main Points/Ideas'. Early fluent readers are encouraged to summarize.

Summarizing is choosing what is important and paraphrasing it and telling it concisely in an ordered sequence and in a way that it makes sense. Readers condense text information into a few important ideas or larger concepts and infer themes.

SYNTHESIZING

Synthesizing is integrating existing knowledge with what is said in a text (literal), what may be meant (interpretive) and then extending (applying) ideas beyond the situation.

By synthesizing children add to their store of knowledge; they combine strategies which may consolidate what they already know or merge new information with existing knowledge, analyse (examine it in parts) to form a core idea, judgement or a particular opinion.

Synthesizing leads readers to understand fresh perspectives; develop new insights, formulate new ideas, make new connections and meaning.

QUESTIONING

Proficient readers are actively engaged in asking questions as they read and search for answers. For example, they may challenge information in the text, the author's purpose, and their connections with the content. As they ask wondering questions, for example, about a character's motives, a particular twist in the plot, or an element of the author's style, definitions of words, they focus more on the meaning of the piece they are reading.

Closed questions are just that, there is only one answer and those answers are literal, *Tell me what the story is about?,* the answer is stated in the text.

There are questions readers ask that indicate they are confused or not understanding aspects and need them to be clarified, *What was meant by..?*

Open-ended questions lead us to seek out further information/research; leads to inferential thinking, they allow discussion to happen. This type of question generally does not have a final answer, but the ensuing discussion and the exchange of perspectives open readers' minds to possibilities.

A teacher's role is to ask questions that:

- give readers a purpose to read;
- prompt readers to think;
- guide readers through the investigative process;
- will not always have one right answer; there may be many answers;
- cause readers to ponder and wonder;
- challenge readers to rethink their judgements and opinions;
- allow viable interpretations;
- cause multiple perspectives;
- stimulate discussion, conversation, debate;
- may require further research.

KNOWING ABOUT VARIOUS TEXT/LANGUAGE STRUCTURES

In order for readers to predict, infer, retell, determine important information and summarize they need to have prior knowledge of text structures and the type of language that is part of those structures (e.g. procedures *command verbs,* narratives, *action verbs, saying verbs* expositions *noun groups, connectives).*

Knowledge about text structures helps a reader make associations and recognise patterns. A reader with **no** preconceived ideas about the text structure will find predicting and all other comprehension strategy use difficult. But a reader with prior knowledge of text structures will be able to anticipate the flow of content and associated language. Readers need to know that:

- Stories generally orientate readers to the characters and settings, that most stories have a problem (caused by...) and a solution and a 'tie up ending'.

- Information texts also have an orientation (different to narrative), it being an opening statement. Shifts in ideas will be announced by (a) headings, (b) noun groups at the beginning of sentences and paragraphs, and these will be followed by descriptions and particular information.

RETELLING

There is a minor difference between retelling and summarizing. Readers (early and developing) may tell more about what the author has written when retelling: they focus on the literal elements of a text, telling information about the characters, the setting and sequence of events, they may describe the important **and** interesting information the author has related.

Focal point: **Comprehension strategies – example questions to model**

A number of example questions are listed to help teachers view questions that promote the ten comprehension strategies during reading.

You model these questions during Read Aloud, Shared Reading and Guided Reading and the children eventually 'take responsibility' and ask their own questions when reading or working with a small group.

Helpful Hints
Choose one or two questions from each strategy that is/are suitable for the learning needs of your children (figure 6).   **Write these questions on your 'Guided Reading Recording' sheet** (Black line masters *examples* 1,2,3, *blank* 4,5,6, pages 105-110).   **Be flexible as the group may have alternative, relevant thoughts.**

Making Connections/Using Schema -
How is the story like your world?   Have you been in this situation?

Were there places in the story that made you want to laugh, feel good or sad, or related to your life?

Have you had an experience like this?

Do you think you are like the main character?

Can you think of other stories that have a similar rhythm, language?

Have you read a story similar to this story?

Have you read information about this topic before?

Compare this character with the character in …….

Compare the plot with the plot in ………

Compare … theme, setting, author's other work.

Do you know a word that means the same as this word?

Predicting

After looking at the cover, title and pictures, contents page, blurb, 1st page…What do you think this story is about?

What do you think will mostly likely happen next?

What will [X] do when ……………………?

How will the story end?

Contextual clues-
Quoting a sentence or passage What does this word ………….. mean in the sentence?

Visualizing –

During Read Aloud close your eyes when I read this passage and tell what you see?

Based on his/her actions, how would you describe [*character's name*]?

Which descriptions show how [*character's name*] feels?

Making Inferences –

Infer why the author called the story …..

What do you think the author meant ....?

How can you tell that ....?

Where does it give a clue in this paragraph what the theme might be?

If the main character gets into that situation again, what do you think [character's name] will do?

What could happen to the character after the story ends?

What is the author of this poem trying to tell us?

The author does not say so, but what can you assume .... ?

[Quoting a sentence or passage] infer what might the meaning be?

What were the main character's motives?

As a result of ....

Determining Main Points/Ideas –

What is this story/passage .... mainly about? Let's choose a title for this passage.

The main thing that happens in this passage is ....

Which of these .... is the best title for this chapter/passage?

The main idea of this article is ....

What is this invitation/advertisement for?

Which of the following sentences best explains the point of the passage?

What is the main idea in the story? What makes you think that?

What words/phrases explain the point of the passage ?

What did the author want you to think about?

What are the main facts of this information?

Is .... a fact or an opinion?

Summarizing -

Interpret the theme?

Tell the main parts of the story.

What is the main problem in the story? How was the problem solved?

Tell the main facts.

What is this issue about?

Synthesizing and Analysing –

Did the story end the way you expected it to, or was it a surprise? Why? What other way could the story end?

Knowing the story to this point can you imagine what happened to the character after the story ended?

Did you think the author resolved the problem effectively? Was there another way?

Was the title the author gave the book an interesting/appropriate title …….? What title would you suggest?

How did you learn about the character? Is it what she does or what she says? Give examples from the text.

Is the resolution satisfying? What would you suggest?

What are minor characters' roles in the life of the main character?

Would the story be different if it were told by one of the minor characters?

Based on [*name of character's*] actions, how would you describe this character? What made the character important?

Changing any one of the below how does it effect the story? How would you make the story more dramatic, humorous, scary?

- settings, e.g. another time, place
- parts of the story e.g. ending, beginning events
- character behaviour
- poem into a narrative

Does the author have an opinion? Do you have an opinion?

Perspectives – your opinion, what changes would you suggest?

What can you learn from this? Is there anything that was omitted?

Questioning/Wondering – thinking focuses

What solution would you suggest?

Why did the character act like he did?

Perspectives - how character felt/how you, the reader felt/pretend you are character.

Compare/contrast the character, plot, theme, setting, author's other work (key words are generally, *most, like, different, alike, similar).*

What is real? What is fantasy?

What language/vocabulary stimulates feelings? Mood? Imagery? Memorable phrases?

How will the story unfold or information be presented?

What will happen to the character after the story is concluded?

What was the character like? What made the character important?

What was the theme? Compare sameness and differences in stories.

What part did you like best? Thought interesting? Humorous? Why do you think that way?

For clarification, "Don't understand ... how can I find out?"

Understanding Text/Language Structures of various genres –

Sequencing -
What happened ….first, last, in the middle?
When did …………………..happen?

Grammatical structures/Language features -
(Explicit teaching of these during Share Reading, deconstruction of texts).

Cause and effect relationships -
………………………happened because ……………………
The main character acted like he /she did in order to …………………………
As a result of ……………………
Why did [X] do ……………………………What was the effect?

What was the cause/effect of ...? (E.g. I forgot to set my alarm clock, so I was late for school).

Author's writing style –
What is the author's purpose? To persuade, give information, to describe, to entertain
What did you notice about his or her style of writing?
Compare this book to others you've read by this author?
How does the author get you interested in the beginning or ending chapters of the book?
How does the author introduce you to the setting?
Could this story have happened in another place?
How does the author introduce you to the characters?
What technique does the author use to draw you into the story? Cause tension?
Does the author use particular language, for example, spoken dialogue, language that provokes images?
Does the author use unusual vocabulary?

What figurative language does the author use? Language - that stimulates feelings, mood, imagery, memorable phrases.

Non-fiction structures -
What do information texts have … contents, headings, index, glossaries, diagrams, labels etc? How do these graphics help understanding?
Compare structures common to explanations and common to expositions.
Which passage expresses an opinion/fact?

Retelling – Recalling

Tell the plot.

Tell the main parts of the story, beginning, middle, ending.

Where was this story set?

Who are the main characters?

Tell the facts about ……..

Which of these events happened ….first, last, in the middle?

What happens after/before ……. an event, or a step in a process?

After [*character's name*] did …………, what did he/she do next?

Figure 6

Focal point: **So, how** do **these comprehension strategies fit into a Guided Reading lesson?**

Keeping on the comprehension track during Guided Reading (Figure 7).

FIVE PARTS OF GUIDED READING:

Before sitting with Guided Reading group	Teacher carefully chooses the text based on: ✓ support focus or teaching point mostly generated from the day before reading; ✓ most they can read, one or two challenges so learning can occur; ✓ *Information from Running Records/Miscue analysis/comprehension questions;* ✓ a topic or text structure being studied in the classroom; ✓ If possible children's interests.
Introduction (story orientation)	Group sits in front of the teacher who supports when necessary – prompts, confirms, challenges, responds. ***Comprehension strategies:*** . ***Making connections*** . ***Predicting*** . ***Knowing text/language structures*** . ***Questioning*** It is most important that children are orientated to the storyline before they read. They predict and become familiar with the story (or information). Begin by reading the title and looking at the cover, *"What do you think this story could be about?"* Orientate students to unfamiliar text and language structures and vocabulary (especially technical words found in non-fiction). **(Note: If necessary, always familiarize readers to unfamiliar character names during orientation and reading. Voice a connection, "Do you know anyone with the name...? This character has the same name.").** Refer to the strategy taught yesterday: *how did you work out that word?* If possible, choose a book with the same word so they consolidate the strategy, *"What comprehension strategy did you use yesterday to help you understand the story?"*

	Early fluent readers, read blurb on back of book, contents, look at the pictures. Read 1 or 2 pages and predict the storyline themselves. You can give them something to look for when reading (gives them a purpose for reading) for example, *When you read determine what caused Gus to want to take the action he did.*
During reading	*Levels **1-9*** children read aloud. *Levels **1-5*** read the book 2-3 times in the session (each time they reread their fluency improves and their understandings are refined, confirmed, extended). Each child sets his or her own pace. Remind them to listen to themselves when they are reading. As they experience a challenge you teach a strategy to decode or understand (or tell and then teach after the reading). After approx *level **10***, children read silently. You tap each child on the shoulder to indicate you want them to read a part of the text aloud (check fluency). Have small post-it notes to place under a word that they cannot read. Deal with it after the discussion. Be aware that if they have difficulty with more than three words they are reading at too hard a level. ***Comprehension strategies as they read:*** . ***Continuing Predicting, Making connections;*** . ***Knowing text/language structures;*** . ***Visualizing;*** . ***Inferring;*** . ***Determining main points;*** . ***Confirming/using 'fix-up' strategies;*** . ***Questioning, clarifying, recall.***
After reading discussion	Pre prepare a question(s.) Have a focus, but be prepared to change direction if a child, group takes the initiative. Children do most of the talking. Listen and observe. Take note of a comprehension strategy you may need to model at the end of the discussion or during the next day's introduction. ***Comprehension strategies:*** . ***Retelling or summarizing*** . ***Determining main points*** . ***Inferring*** . ***Questioning – open-ended, children posing questions*** . ***Synthesizing/analysing/making judgements/conclusions***

| **Re-Reading (early and developing readers)** | Children re-read the book (as part of independent activity) that day and any future days. |

Figure 7

During Guided Reading teachers will continually make their own professional decisions based on their knowledge of the Guided Reading process. Guided Reading sessions are flexible with conversation about stories and pertinent information being the emphasis.

4

> *"Teacher reads the story before the group reads the story."*

Chapter focal point

Book Orientation

'Let struggling readers relax when reading. Read marvellous literature to these children, repeat the stories. The more familiar they are with the story the more easily they will be able to read, all by their clever selves' (Mem Fox. 2001).

Mem Fox's sentiments are commendable and making children familiar with stories and information does happen in the classroom during Read Aloud and Shared Reading and re-reading during Independent Activities/Tasks. I am also in favour of struggling readers involved in Inquiry, share reading with the teacher. Relating this sentiment to Guided Reading ... put this into the unsure basket.

Certainly, some early readers and delayed readers would benefit from hearing the story beforehand. Rehearsal time may improve reading comprehension and fluency and ultimately increase reading success. A teacher and early reader may take turns reading the text. As the child's confidence and competence increases, he or she reads independently longer sections and then moves to independently reading all of the text.

Focal point: **Book Orientation**

In Reading Recovery an interactive, well-thought out **book orientation** is emphasized. It allows the child to read most of the book independently. (For early readers I have, during the orientation, verbally repeated lines but not brought the associated print to the children's attention).

Orientation to the story/information happens at all levels of reading - early, developing, early fluent (even Book Clubs, see Liz Simon's *Thinkers and Performers Bringing Critical Thinking Alive*, chapters 8 and 9, 2010). The time spent on orientating readers to ideas, unknown text/language structures and vocabulary gives students the support to be able to work more independently when reading.

The word anticipation is fairly well used in this book in relation to comprehension strategies. I see the notion of ANTICIPATION as the core of a book introduction and, furthermore, a child's ability to read independently. Anticipation is the consequence of connecting ideas in the text with the reader, predicting and knowing text and language structures. A reader may think, *I have had this experience or know about a similar happening so I expect something similar, I am pretty sure this will happen, I am familiar with how stories or information are arranged and I know what story language or factual language sounds like so I guess this text will be similar.*

Skilled book introductions require planning and practise!

Orientation to texts focus on children seeing **patterns**. A child who has an existing knowledge framework of ideas presented in story books and of typical patterns of texts are able to predict what will happen in texts that have:

- repetitive patterns, cumulative patterns, rhythm and rhyming patterns
- time sequence patterns; where each episode relates to the one before
- main character, problem and solution patterns
- the pattern of a general statement with descriptions that expands on the generalization.

A reader knowing about language structures (punctuation, grammar) will know when to pause, when the word is 'were' and not 'was'; what connectors and conjunctions are used to make texts cohesive.

If this knowledge framework is not obvious, teachers make it obvious when orientating children to the substance of unfamiliar books.

Returning to the teacher reading the story prior to the new reader or the delayed reader. Reading instead of giving a skilled orientation to the book, will depend on the teacher's judgement based on what she knows about the child's abilities and self-confidence. But that approach has to be temporary, as strategies such as predicting, making connections, knowing text structures and language structures must be internalized and utilized by each reader in order to predict and monitor their reading; to make informed decisions as they read and become independent readers.

5

The term 'picture walk' has become synonymous with introducing (orientating) readers to the story.

Visual support – pictures to discuss

A picture walk is when the child looks at the pictures prior to reading the book in order to acquire a general idea of what the story might be about. My reservation is that the 'picture walk' proceeds as such, "What is happening?" turn the page, "What is happening now" turn the page, "What is happening now" and so on. This view of 'picture walks' assume illustrations are only used to help read the words. 'Picture walks' tend to place illustrations in the service of written language...viewing text and illustrations as two separate meaning systems, ignoring the interplay between them, for example do the pictures complement the story or extend the story?

Preferably, the term 'picture walk' is ignored, instead saying, "Oooh! I wonder what this story is about?" and then continue to converse about aspects in the illustrations. Knowing that the teacher and children explore meanings through visualizing... with illustrations already on the page they find meaning through the visual interpretation of the illustrator.

It is great when teachers show obvious, genuine enthusiasm when introducing the stories, "I just love the stories about 'Little Bear' he gets into such troublesome situations; you may have had similar experiences to his" (making a connection when exploring the picture). "Look at what he is doing in this picture... is he...?" (inferring as the picture is explored). Children also like to follow characters and read books where these characters appear both in the illustrations and the text.

Focal point: **Visual support – pictures to discuss**

Probing pictures in texts sets the stage for successful independent reading. Teacher and children discuss what is happening in the pictures and anticipate what might happen further on, "This picture shows the character jumping the creek, I wonder how this will be part of the story?" (Predicting as the picture is explored).

The focus is upon the construction of meaning made by the children as they integrate pictures, their prior understandings and experiences and print. Initially, controlled by the teacher, analysing the pictures enables young readers to insert their own ideas and later take on this strategy themselves.

Pictures are an integral part of picture books; their enchanting appearance motivates and stimulates imagination. Books used for instructional reading should have the same qualities as good picture books; illustrated and written to bring children reading success, understanding and the desire to read. I know artists spend hours drawing, re-drawing and polishing their work with the aim to push the meanings in the texts along.

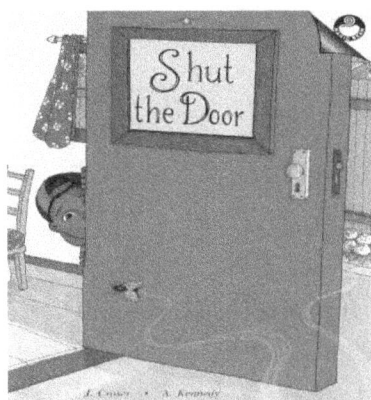

Not only are readers affected by the pictures in fiction books, but children mulling over the diagrams, maps and other graphics in information books add to understanding. Many times I have observed children reading the continuous print of a non-fiction but not the captions. In the introduction (orientation) teachers draw children's attention to the preciseness of graphics and the use of these extra cues to help decode and learn about the topic.

There is so much to learn about the context just from referring to the cover illustration and the first few pictures within the text. Setting the scene is especially important for new readers, English as a Second Language readers and delayed learners. It activates schema in order to maximize comprehension. A teacher by inviting children to respond to the pertinent parts of the cover illustration establishes the topic, title and characters and sometimes the plot at the outset. Pictures can also help understanding of text and language (syntactic) structures as they read.

All pictures do not have to be explored; especially consider leaving the final pages and allow the suspense to build as the children wonder how the story will end.

Your aim is to have children using strategies such as scanning pictures quickly to predict and connect with the texts; add to the mood of the story. Noun groups and some verbs are shown in pictures as are relationships of objects (e.g. a ball hit over the fence), settings and sequencing of ideas.

When children read books with less and less pictures they assume the role of the 'illustrator' and visualize their own settings, plots, character actions and information. Developing readers look for text clues; they do not always refer to or have picture cues to hypothesize or clarify words and understanding.

6

Control of discourse remains very much in hands of teachers – their utterances are longer than students.

Developing child discussion

When working with some teachers introducing Book Clubs, I had to continually remind them to allow the children to talk. I would often turn to the Book Club group and ask them what they thought of the teacher's idea. The children's eyes inevitably would turn to the teacher trying to guess what was expected of them. Children showed little signs of experience in conducting their own discussions. Furthermore, students nearly always referred their query to the teacher and the teacher would inevitably answer. It would have been appropriate in this scenario for the teacher to refer the query back to the group, *I would like to hear what you think.*

This can happen during discussions in Guided Reading. Because children are often reticent talkers in learning situations, teachers ask a child by name to respond, all children's eyes are on the teacher rather than looking at their peers for reactions; their thoughts and opinions. Maybe teachers need to alter the emphasis in Guided Reading discussions to allowing more responsibility to pass to students. Children may not have the perfect answers but they will never develop their thinking and discussion techniques if a teacher is thinking and speaking for them.

There is the point, also, that too much talk and attention to detail by the teacher can dismember the story and mislead inexperienced young readers.

David Skidmore (2003) contributes to the study of teacher-pupil talk by concluding, that during discussion he observed that teachers:

- Rarely ask authentic questions;
- Normally control turn-taking by nominating the next speaker;
- Keep a tight grip on the topic of conversation; and
- Do most of the talking.

Robin Alexander's 2004 study *Towards Dialogic Teaching: Rethinking Classroom Talk* (as cited in Annie Fisher, 2008. P.23) found that even when students answer a question, the answer is not explored or expanded on by the teacher; there was 'little teaching of inferential comprehension and none of evaluative strategies ... [no] opportunity to make and justify judgements. No follow up with cognitively demanding probes'.

Focal point: **Developing child discussion**

To help children interact with their peers and deflect their attention away from the teacher, ask questions that cause readers to expand their thinking (Figure 8).

Keeping focused *What is it that puzzles you?* *What did you find interesting?* *Why do you agree or disagree with X* **Reasons** *Why did you say that?* *What reasons do you have?* **Examples** *Can anyone give an example of that?* **Counter examples** *Can you think of a case or a time when that wouldn't work?* **Distinctions** *How is that different to what X said?* **Consistency** *Is that the same as you said earlier?* *Does that agree with what was said earlier?* **Alternatives** *How else could we think about that?* *What if someone said ...?* *There are some people who think that...*	**When inferencing, implying or making assumptions.** *How do you know that?* *What have you based that on?* *What can we assume from that comment?* *What does that tell us?* *What follows from what X said?* *Can anyone think of how that might have happened?* **Testing** *How could you work out if that was true?* **Information gathering** *What do you know about that?* **Summarising** *What have you found out?* *Where has the group got to?* **Clarification** *What do you mean by that?* *Can anyone help X explain that more clearly?* **Relevance** *How does that help?*

Figure 8

It takes a lot of practise to operate this way but in any discussion situation this approach allows meaningful and critical conversations to take place.

A teacher's role is to allow students to confer with each other and speculate about their current reading; develop and justify their opinions and perspectives; develop analytical and critical responses. Teachers talk only when there is a need to model, to quickly expand children's thoughts and after the discussion to give explicit feedback about their performance. Teacher's talk is sociable, short and to the point.

Helpful Hints

1. First of all train children in collaborative discussion right from level 1; teach children **group behaviour that is conducive to successful discussion** e.g. eye contact, taking turns, listening to each other and most importantly from approximately level 10 children learn to **'chain conversations'** (Skidmore, 2003) **e.g. *That was interesting. Why did you say that? I didn't quite understand, can you give some more detail? I thought almost the same but then you said...;***

2. Plan and ask one or two **open-ended questions** as models for children to adopt;

3. Allow **children to explore alternative perspectives** where they consider all viewpoints and logical inferences are deduced (including unfamiliar words), ideas are interpreted within the context of what has been read.

7

"Guided Reading is a set of routine steps to work through."

Chapter focal point

Developing enthused, independent reading and thinking

The view that "Guided Reading is a set of routine steps" may indicate that the teacher does not truly know what Guided Reading involves. Teachers may be executing Guided Reading at a superficial level. It may include Guided Reading being a sporadic or a last minute event. It may possibly be that Guided Reading is seen as 'hear them read, ask them the same closed questions each week' - questions that involve recall only, "Who was the main character?", "What happened?" and so on. Literal recall privileges the text over the reader and their thinking.

It may be teachers have an almost 'outside the skin' viewpoint of Guided Reading. I mean by this that they come with questions from a publisher's resource or questions **and answers** printed on card; that by referring to a prepared script there is no spontaneous, thoughtful and relevant decisions being made by the teacher there and then. They treat reading instruction merely as an exercise that they are in control of.

Focal point: **Developing enthused, independent reading and thinking**

I will discuss four points that discourage thoughts about the implementation of Guided Reading being routine.

> **Teachers engender the feeling that reading is a delight and discussing what has been read is stimulating**.

What is motivating and engaging for the teacher and consequently the children is that she is enthused about what is going to be read, is excited about the wonderful reading and thoughts the children have and relishes the progress children make during Guided Reading. Teachers valuing the hypothetical nature of text-related talk will create an environment where participants feel at ease to voice their opinions, clarify their confusions and ask and answer a myriad of questions and laugh at humorous aspects.

The instructional aim of Guided Reading is to make children independent readers and thinkers of text and this is no easy task.

Teachers are supporting children to develop reading and thinking; ways of exploring texts they would not be able to manage unaided.

During Guided Reading a teacher's mind is continually active. There are so many decisions that a teacher makes; no two Guided Reading sessions are the same if the learning needs, styles of the readers and problems that arise are being catered for and, furthermore, teachers are forever building bridges between what is known and what is new and judging when and the best way of transferring the responsibility to children.

As the Guided Reading session proceeds teachers are thinking, "Which strategy will I demonstrate?" "What will I reinforce?", "How will I show the student how they use/take on this strategy?", "Is the child approximately reading independently at that level?", "Will I move to a new stage? for example, from now on I want them to be able to orientate themselves to stories." "What questions will this text allow me to ask to put in play higher order thinking?"

It was found in the study by Alexander et al (as cited in Fisher, Annie. 2008) that teachers need to ask genuine exploratory questions, so a teacher guiding children during a Guided Reading session has to be thinking whether he is developing in readers the ability to ask inferential questions and use evaluative strategies (e.g. giving readers opportunity to make and justify judgements) or whether the readers should now be using these strategies themselves during their discussion; using the strategies without prompting,

Good you really thought about what the character is doing to infer what he is like as a person.

The examples below of explicit language when working with Guided Reading groups also shows the judgements, the 'twists and turns', teachers make and take as they work with different groups. When children are reading, all sorts of thinking and learning is happening; all sorts of teaching decisions and teacher responses are happening. This requires that teachers are knowledgeable about the best possible approaches to impart to children.

A knowledgeable teacher is a decisive teacher. A knowledgeable teacher uses explicit language. Knowledge, decisiveness and explicit language, take away any thoughts of Guided Reading being routine.

Examples of the decisions teachers make

BEFORE READING

Introduction to new texts:

- ○ *You may want the reader to distinguish between fact and imagination... this story is about ... The characters are ... I wonder if it is a fairy tale or will it be a true story?*
- ○ *You may want the reader to be aware of a strategy...What do you think you may need to think about as you read this story/information?*

Children gaining more experience, begin them on the path to predicting before they read:

- ○ You say: *You look at the pictures yourselves to page...? As you look at some of the pictures, say to yourself, I think this happening ... I think this could happen/or I think this will happen next... I think the ending will be... I think the main idea will be ...You orient yourselves to the story.*
- ○ *What strategies did you use to get to know what the story may be about?*
- ○ *You may decide that the reader orientates himself to the story...When you handle a new book you have been reading the title, what else have you been doing?*
  (The answer, *I predict what the story will be about then I connect what I think the book is about with my experiences and I expect a certain text structure and certain language structures because the book is a story. This helps me to read because I know ahead what the story pattern is*).
- ○ *Look at the cover and say to yourself, I think this information is about...*
- ○ A teacher makes the decision about how long they allow children to think about predictions. They reflect on whether all children in the group know what predictions are? They ascertain whether their predictions are logical. Have the clues on the page initiated some imaginative suggestions or has the child repeated the title only and this has been accepted or does the teacher reply, *Yes, the title says that, but this story is about more things happening. Look at the cover it has ... What other things could happen...?*
- ○ *A key word in the title is 'ghost'; what do you know about ghosts?*
- ○ *A teacher makes connections...From your knowledge of stories you have read about ghosts and how stories work, what could the author be writing about ghosts?*
- ○ You may decide that it is an opportune time for the children in the group to turn to a partner and talk about their predictions.
- ○ While they are doing this you listen, observe and note their responses and give explicit feedback, *Good, you are really looking at the cover and thinking about what the story could be about.*

A teacher introducing a chapter book to early fluent readers may begin by asking:

- ○ *What do you do when you choose books?*

Any action the children have not related the teacher may explicitly tell, *When choosing a book you read the title, look at the cover pictures, read the 'blurb' on the cover, look at the pictures yourselves, read the first page.* At an appropriate time you expect children to take on the strategy.

DURING READING

Most of the reading done by early fluent readers is away from the group they can use sticky notes:

- Quickly annotate on a post-it note, *Feelings about this piece so far. The implication of the information just read? What X may mean? Note where you went for help... the glossary or was it the context clues? Place a sticky note to mark something you did not understand or cannot read. Note on sticky notes open ended questions - what could, how might, what if, what do you think about etc?* You instruct: *Mark with a sticky note the passage you need to clarify – be prepared to read the passage aloud.*
- *Ask yourself. What important information do I need to know and remember?*
- The teacher reinforces topic sentences... Where is the main idea generally started?

AFTER READING

Shifting the onus to the group:

- *What did you think about as you read the story/information? What strategies did you use to think about the story?*
- *It is good to review the last page of a previous chapter to help you remember what has happened so far.*
- *How did you establish the main idea(s) in the last chapter? How was this expressed by the author? How did Chapter X end?*
- *If you are having difficulty remembering, stop and ask yourself questions, e.g. what has happened so far? Why? How might? Where could?*
- The teacher wants the the reading group to prepare for discussion... *As you read, place a self stick note to mark something interesting to share with a partner.*
- You make explicit: *Today after you read, you will sit with a partner and retell the main ideas (of the story or information) to your partner.*
- *You can help your partner, if you think an important part has been left out.*

Children take on talk themselves

They begin the conversation, find evidence in the text to confirm their argument and listen carefully to each other. As has been stated in the introduction this collaborative approach moves away from the normal question and answer format; the teacher, rather than ask question upon question, responds to children's talk in a more non-committal way **'maybe'**, **'I wonder'** and encourages the children to talk to each other.

Making meaning is happening as children read (it is not something that happens after a child has read) and to help transpose that thinking into verbal responses teachers prepare by jotting one or two open-ended questions (or observations) to ask their group. The teacher does not have to ask their prepared questions (the discussion may go in a different direction) but this preparation allows the teacher flexibility – will he begin the discussion with his prepared question or is the situation such that the children take on the talk themselves?

The outcome being that every utterance is valued; not only are teachers stimulated but also children enjoy reading and conversing with each other about texts.

Vary the reading

The below case study recounts how this is done.

Case Study #1

The teacher and the class were studying myths; what is real and what is unreal in this type of story. She chose to follow-up on this study in Guided Reading for her level 18 students choosing, 'The Emperor and the Nightingale' by Hans Christian Andersen. To extend their reading and enhance the group's view of myths, she copied from the internet some information about the author, Hans Christian Andersen. In the information piece was mentioned two of his stories, 'The Ugly Duckling' and the 'Little Mermaid'.

After orientating the group to the story 'The Emperor and the Nightingale' (and incidentally, the predictions and connections the children made related to other tales they had read about Emperors and nightingales), she asked them to think and form opinions about what may be real in the story and what is unreal.

They were then asked to expand their independent reading by reading a biography about Hans Christian Andersen and see if they could connect his life with, 'The Emperor and the Nightingale' (Nisbet Bain, 2002).

They also went to Library and read, 'The Ugly Duckling' and the 'Little Mermaid' to compare these with 'The Emperor and the Nightingale'.

While reading they created 1-2 questions or comments about the **three** stories and Andersen's life (if they commented they extended their comments using the phrase ."..what do you think"). As there were sentences the teacher anticipated the children may find hard to decipher the meaning, she reminded them to ask any clarifying questions.

The group came to the discussion with a lot of background information and a lot of interesting ideas. Reading only the book 'The Emperor and the Nightingale' may have restricted conversation.

8

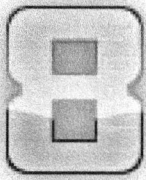

> *Guided Reading turns into Round Robin reading where each child reads aloud a part of the text.*

Guided Reading is children reading the whole text

Variations in Early level reading, Developing level reading, Early Fluent Reading

Many times this comment has dominated views of Guided Reading, "I learnt that it is Round Robin reading when children read in Guided Reading" and in a condensed version of a curriculum document relating to early years literacy this statement about small group independent reading was recorded, *students sit in their groups and each read sections of the book.*

To begin, an explanation of Round Robin reading is necessary, then a comparison with Guided Reading will follow.

Round Robin Reading is oral reading where each child in the class/group takes a turn to read a part (e.g. a paragraph) of the text. Meanwhile, the rest of the class/group silently, supposedly, follows along. ·

Generally, there is no orientation to the story; teachers do not talk about ideas or strategies. Reading keeps moving from one child to the next. Again, supposedly, a short time is allowed for the child to problem solve unfamiliar words on his or her own, but often their peers 'jump in' and say the word for them.

The effect of Round Robin reading on the self esteem of under developed readers cannot be glossed over. Round Robin reading is a *performance* where good readers read fluently, may 'hum' and 'ha' as the poor reader stumbles nervously and embarrassedly through their reading performance.

Another common behaviour of readers during Round Robin reading is for the student to count the number of students before she is due to read; the reader may rehearse that passage beforehand and after the child has read she shuts down, "I have done my performance, I can go off in a dream." You can see how, for many children, comprehension and the love for reading would not happen implementing this type of reading method.

Students, even the better readers, rarely pay attention when it is not their turn to read, often good readers are reading the text and not listening to other readers. No effective reading instruction occurs, except, "You read the wrong word Tom. Josh (a good reader) tell

Tom (the poor reader) what the word is." Further, when Round Robin reading happens the method seems to positively discourage discussion involving deep understanding of the text.

If the time each child spends reading is totalled during Round Robin reading, the old adage "Readers learn to read by reading" flies out the window. Each child spends very little time reading - few minutes, at the most, in a session.

Case Study #2

To Popcorn or not to Popcorn?

A teacher stated online, that she played 'popcorn' during Guided Reading. She states that a reader begins to read then calls 'popcorn' and a child's name and that child continues the reading. She continues to explain that the children are practising reading and are given choices of reading a sentence or up to a paragraph with the more confident readers reading longer.

Although there is a little more spontaneity as regards who would read next, I see this as Round Robin reading using another name.

Focal Point: **Guided Reading is children reading the whole text**

Guided Reading, on the other hand, involves differentiated teaching and learning; it allows all children to read quality texts, to be shown reading strategies, ideas and be participants in lively discussion (refer to information in the Introduction page, 3).

Guided Reading is children **independently reading the whole text**.

Focal Point: **Variations in Early level reading, Developing level reading, Early Fluent Reading**

Guided Reading for different levels of readers has slight variations, for example, Levels 1-9 generally read aloud but from level 10 onwards children read silently. More specifically:

Early readers L 1-9

Children have at least 75% letter knowledge. As I continually explain to teachers, a first fix-up strategy is, "Look at what the word begins with." Without a substantial knowledge of letters children would not be able to respond to this prompt.

The group is approximately 4 students with 10-15 minutes given to each group. (The early books are short and do not require the length of time orienting, reading and discussing that books with more content require). During Shared Reading and Read Aloud, you are beginning to show structures of different texts and the language that accompanies the varied structures. As soon as you think the children are ready, include some simple non-fiction titles and some rhymes /poetry.

During reading:

o   The group sits around you, as children read you note strategies they are using and difficulties they are having and what you will do quickly at the end of their reading or the next day when you first meet (Black line master 4 record sheet, page 108, example Black line master 1 page 105).

o   After the introduction (orientation to the story) each child **reads aloud** in a quiet voice (loud enough for the teacher to hear). They read <u>at the same time</u> but <u>not together</u>. Instead each child sets their own pace, listening to themselves. If they fall into reading along with each other the teacher may stop one of the children and ask, "Tell me what you have read so far?" and then the child continues to read independently without listening to his neighbour. Any child who has difficulty with this sit them alongside you, facing a direction that you can easily look down at their book (as though sitting on a love seat).

o   The first reading is generally followed by some brief teaching (e.g. may return to a particular part of the text where a problem arose). Then the group re-reads the text two more times.

o   From level 1 the emphasis is reading fluently, at least for the 2nd and 3rd reading. If the group is reading at a level they are most successful there should not be too much interruption (1 or 2 strategies shown). PM story books (developed in New Zealand) at this level are wonderful as they support the early reader. They have:

-   A traditional story structure, the main character has a problem, which motivates the reader into finding how the problem is solved and allows the teacher to ask predicting questions e.g. *What will happen next?* Knowing this structure helps children self-correct. PM's have 'happy' endings; they provide opportunities for the development of logical thought and understanding of the cause and the effect of problems.

-   The topics are varied and the stories have characters and episodes that make it easy for the readers to connect to their personal experiences. The picture of an example cover of a PM book bears this out:

- There are a minimum of surprise twists in plots and sentence structures relate to normal spoken English and rhythms of story-telling.

- At each level batches of high frequency words are introduced (no more than 5) and they accumulate and depending on the word, appear at the beginning, middle and ending of sentences (there are few unexpected words).

- They gradually allow children to expand their reading mastery e.g. longer sentences later on.

- They match illustrations with the content and this allows children to use the illustrations as a way into predicting words, maintaining meaning.

- The font is clear, appropriate word and line spacing, and the return sweep is introduced early.

Helpful Hints

- Levels 1-2 (PM Story Starters), children often memorize the sentences. Direct them to the print because as they move up the levels attention to print is essential, *How did you know that word? Because it began with a /t/.*

- From approximately level 5 children do the third re-read away from the teacher with a partner.

- As each member of the group reads the teacher listens and assists if required, remembering that each child must be able to read most of the text.

- Children re-read, re-read <u>silently</u> or to partners (*re-reading is affected by the understandings/behaviour as it <u>refines,</u> <u>confirms,</u> <u>extends</u> the first reading.*

- Finger pointing until word match happens (finger pointing can slow and affect fluency because it inhibits a reader's ability to scan ahead for print information). Instead refer to 'eye-pointing'. *Note:* any child with difficulty following words written in a line would be encouraged to continue finger pointing.

- <u>After a discussion</u> about the story a strategy on one word is shown on a | a | m | small whiteboard e.g. use sound boxes.

- The quick learning of 15 high frequency words happens (see chapter 9, page 61).

- If possible place one copy of the book in baskets specified for each group. These are re-read to a peer or an adult (e.g. parent) during Independent Activities or early morning reading.

Developing readers L 10-20

You can have a group of approx. 6 students, they read silently (see During Reading). From about L15 a Guided Reading session may be 15-20 minutes in length as the texts are generally more lengthy. Longer texts can be read in one or two sessions, remembering you will need time for discussion.

During Reading:

o   The group sits around you, as children read you note strategies they are using and difficulties they are having and what you will do the next day you meet (see Guided Reading example recording, Black line master 2, page 106).

o   After the introduction (orientation to the story) each child reads **silently**. What this looks like is demonstrated by the teacher in the initial sessions. The teacher reads silently, eyes on the book and mouth closed. The children mirror the same behaviour.

o   A touch on the shoulder by the teacher or some other sign indicates that a reader reads aloud from the point he or she has read to. You check fluency, what strategies are being used, whether there are difficulties with the level they are reading. When you move to the next reader, the previous reader goes into silent mode and the 'new' reader 'reads aloud'.

o   Prepare some generic task cards for children if they are waiting for their peers to finish reading. For example, 'Find a word you do not know'. 'Find its meaning in the dictionary'. 'Go to a part in the story you really like and analyse it'.

o   <u>After the discussion</u> a strategy, mostly verbalized, on **one** problem word, only, is <u>demonstrated</u> .

o   After the Guided Reading session, the group can re-read in a quiet area in the classroom (some large cushions may be appropriate); a following task will be indicated on the Task Board (so no explaining should happen). Independent responses to the text are manipulative tasks or generic sheets/task cards (Black line masters 7-14, pages 111-118) or draw/write in your journal some aspect of the story or information).

Early Fluent readers

Early Fluent Readers are 'somewhat' independent readers. These readers have reached level 21; they have a broad reading (and writing) vocabulary and are using comprehension strategies fairly consistently.

Early Fluent readers read a variety of texts – they read literature (including poetry) and non-fiction (topics that capture their interest and imagination or match the Inquiry happening in class).

You can work with 6-8 students for 10 minutes introducing the text and later 10-15 minutes discussion.

During reading:

o The group sits around you as you orientate the group to the text. The orientation takes the form of 'reading around the text' (the title, contents, 'blurb' etc.) and the group make predictions then you may talk about the structure of the piece, any twists in the plot/information, looking at illustrations, diagrams, glossary, making connections with the group's knowledge and experiences.

o You may orientate the group to the **first few pages and STOP at logical parts**, for example, *In the first two pages, there is the usual introduction of the character and setting, On page 4 the author has begun to build tension with the suggestion that there is a big problem going to beset the main character. Look closely at what the character says.*

o Or you could say, *Read to page 4 and find out where...? Read to page 6 and as you read, note what language the author uses to describe the environment? Read to page 8 and find out why...? Find and read the part that describes......?*

o Non-fiction (even some fiction) may require 3-4 Guided Reading sessions (see chapter 12, page 83, 'Typical Guided Reading' non-fiction).

o After the introduction (orientation), the group (I will call them **A**) continues reading, silently, in a quiet area of the classroom. You may have given a thinking question before they read and they use this to write a note about, for example, *Find the problem..., Infer the author's message* or they have small post-its to place against unknown words, mark a point to clarify or share with the group in the next session, or they may complete 'Non-Fiction Notes Sheet' (Black line master 12, page 116).

o Full critical discussion does not happen until the complete text is read (the last reading, they prepare 1-3 open ended questions to stimulate discussion.

o While Group A is independently reading you will be guiding another reading group (I will call this group **B**).

o When any group finishes reading they 'hook' into the Task Board and begin the stated tasks for their particular group, for example, word study, book review in journal, continuing research project, looking for word meanings in dictionary and always spelling – why? Spelling adds to readers developing vocabulary.

- Group A indicates to the teacher when **all** have completed the reading and a time is scheduled for discussion (perhaps, the next day). I give members of each group book-marks and when they return them I know they are ready to form their discussion group. The discussion is exploratory and in-depth.

- The teacher observes the discussion, notes behaviour (thinking and participatory) and gives explicit feedback.

9

> *To read fluently a child must read at a fast rate.*

Chapter focal points
Phrasing
Repeated readings and reading fluency
Wide Vocabulary
Recording vocabulary development

I have been guilty of, "Hurry up you need to read faster" knowing that fluency is not about reading faster but about the student's ability to read effortlessly and not linger over decoding words.

Reading fluently is a student reading smoothly with few errors and self-corrections; the reader does not stop to work out words, instead the reader focuses on meaning and understanding, which in turn assists the reader to predict unfamiliar words (perhaps confirming by quickly looking at the visual aspects e.g. what the word begins with).

Good readers rarely sound out letter-by-letter, instead they predict unknown words by putting into play their prior knowledge of the content they are reading, their knowledge of book language and having a wide vocabulary and using these sources simultaneously (Mem Fox, 2001).

Less fluent readers focus their attention primarily on decoding individual words, their reading is jagged, word-for-word reading, they have little attention left to remember the story or information let alone comprehend and interpret the content. Readers who are painfully sounding out words or reading word on word are using this one strategy to the detriment of meaning.

Reading at an appropriate level, where there is only 1 challenge (early readers) and 1-2 challenges (developing readers) greatly assists fluency and comprehension.

Focal point: **Phrasing**

When children are not reading fluently the teacher models phrased reading. Rather than read word-on-word, readers who are having difficulty reading fluently, are taught to clump a number of words together.

During Shared Reading of poetry, say, children are encouraged to read in phrases. You can write the phrases on cards to show how readers cluster parts of the text. Reinforce this then in Guided Reading by reading poems that can be divided into phrases.

Fluency is worked on right at the beginning of a child reading at school. Model how to read fluently … read like you talk, *Listen to me as I read this phrase/sentence, now you read like that.* Read phrases rather than word by word. *Let's read this smoothly. Listen how I group words together* (frame with your hand). *Why does it make more sense/sounds better that way? Listen to how I read, I don't stop at the end of every line. I keep reading until the punctuation tells me to stop or pause. Let's try that page again and see how we move our eyes immediately to the next line. If the story is about ……… then this word could be…* all the time asking does this make sense?

Children who can automatically read a 'string' of words, predict words and quickly scan pictures and look at parts of words to confirm predictions generally develop smoother, expert reading, so essential for reading for meaning; they are able to concentrate more fully on thinking about the story.

Focal point: **Repeated readings and reading fluency**

Repeated readings happen as part of the Guided Reading session (levels 1-5). Level 6 to approximately level 15 children reread their books as an 'after Guided Reading' activity. Some readers at Level 17+ and all early Fluent readers re-read to complete a task. Each time a child **re-reads** they act differently on the text; they are more at ease, ready to internalize their strategies. With each re-reading, reading is more fluent.

As well children can re-read their books during Independent Reading or if the school has an ample supply they take their books home to re-read (remembering that Guided Reading material is precious and needs to be always on hand for teachers).

Reader's Theatre

Vary the re-reading process for developing, early and fluent readers by implementing Reader's Theatre. Reader's Theatre happens during Independent Activities. A 'down-to–earth' article about Reader's Theatre has been written by Margery Hertzberg (2009). She stated that 'the focus is on how the text is to be read'. The children initially read a play during Guided Reading (or a narrative made into a play during Shared Writing could be read).

Margery Hertzberg emphasises that Reader's Theatre is not a performance (there are no stage sets or costumes) and children read the script rather than memorize lines (in fact, they re-read and re-read!). By taking the roles of the characters children read with expression and may even add lines of their own. Further, they gain insight about character behaviour, plots – cause and effect, problem and solution - and other aspects because of the role-taking and repetitive reading. As a follow on to Reader's Theatre, children could debate or give different interpretations or select an excerpt to discuss (Hertzberg suggests an excerpt to see how the author portrays a moment of high tension).

Reader's Theatre is perfect for differentiating reading tasks. You could imagine a child who is not a confident reader repeating certain lines and later on, take other roles. A more confident reader can take a more 'modelling' role. As each member in the group reads his lines, all members of the group follow the script. This in turn improves word recognition. Reader's Theatre fosters a different atmosphere, more purpose than Round Robin reading or Popcorn!

Repeated reading is important in learning to read and Reader's Theatre provides this opportunity in a purposeful way.

Role play

Role Play helps children view characters and issues from different viewpoints. Children re-read and interpret in their own words. Readers could think about the behaviour, traits and issues through voices, for example: people involved in a contentious industry (e.g. whale industry) – environmentalists, politicians, consumers of whale meat, industry members, writers about the industry. Are female/male views different? Do people's ages make a difference, do different times make a difference (100 years ago as compared to now).

Other re-reading activities could be:

o Read as if you were planning notes for an illustrator.
o Which character do you feel you know the best? Read the book again to see what you can find out about that character.
o As you re-read, think which incident had the most impact on the story line.
o As you re-read, think about the techniques the author uses to create mood, tension and/or pace, portray characters, set the scene without long explanations.
o Write what you think the significance of ... was
o Reread the introduction and glossary and think how much information you were given before you began reading. How did this influence your purpose for reading or the way you read?

Focal point: **Wide Vocabulary**

Mem Fox (2001) mentions a **wide vocabulary**. Knowing the meaning of words, using strategies quickly to work out words; building a wide vocabulary of words greatly assists fluency and hence, comprehension.

Direct attention to certain words is part of a Guided Reading session. For example, in the **introduction** (orientation) the teacher may surmise that a word in the text may be new to the readers so she pronounces the word and asks, *What does it mean? Listen to the sentence and predict its meaning.* And after reading, *How important to the text is that word? What difference does that one word make to overall meaning?*

Introduce the meaning of words in the text by predicting or inferring words flowing from the phrases and sentences **not** as individual words.

Helpful Hints
Provide opportunities for children to hear complex words within sentences before reading: ○ Words not found in illustrations ○ Words where the meaning is unknown ○ Unknown names ○ Intentionally repeat one particular sentence pattern (unfamiliar syntax) which is crucial to the story structure ○ Create opportunities to rehearse literary language

These practices of widening the reading and understanding of vocabulary and language, is different to doing word studies.

It is important that new/early readers quickly learn 15 high-frequency words and know them automatically in and out of context. The quicker children learn high-frequency words (a word a day **from their Guided Reading**) the more easily they are able to monitor their own reading and become fluent readers, forming a base for making word analogies (e.g. relationship of onset and rime – **m**um, **m**at, **we**, **he**, **w**ent **sent**). Within 3 weeks of participation in Guided Reading (level 1), children would have learned and used strategies, such as hearing sounds in words, looking at tricky parts, small words within words (see page 26 'Fix-up' strategies or Liz Simon's *Strategic Spelling, 2004*).

After the Guided Reading discussion, you model a strategy on a high frequency word, for example, *went*, hearing sounds in words, saying the word slowly and showing it in boxes, either letter by letter or the rhyming approach:

w	e	n	t

w	ent

Materials: The teacher always brings to Guided Reading a small white board and a set of magnetic letters in a compartmentalized tray.

Hearing sounds in words can be shown on the whiteboard.

Analogies are made by moving magnetic letters

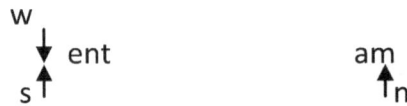

w
↓ ent   am
s↑   ↑n

Both hearing and <u>looking</u> (e.g. *the, was*) is emphasized as strategies for the children to use.

This is a most effective activity in the classroom to promote the quick learning of high frequency words!

This activity replicates the **practising of new words** that happens in Reading Recovery. After the strategy (e.g. hearing sounds in words) is shown, the group moves to a special table on which has been placed a sand tray, plastic letters, paper/pen/scissors, and a white or chalk board (figure 8). For a week you need to support the group by staying with them ensuring they quickly finish each task and return to the group's designated desk.

The group rotates around the table completing the four practising locations. The child at the sand tray practises writing the word *went* 5 times in the sand, the child at the plastic letters location, makes and breaks the word *went* 5 times, the child using paper and scissors writes the word *went* and cuts it as the teacher has modelled, then makes and breaks 3 times, the child using the white board writes the word *went* in each corner and in the middle.

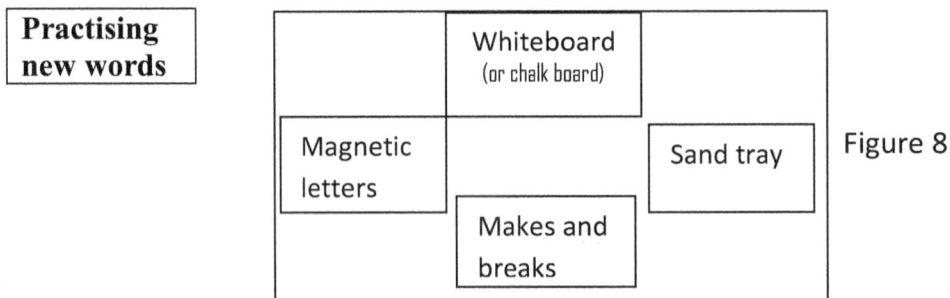

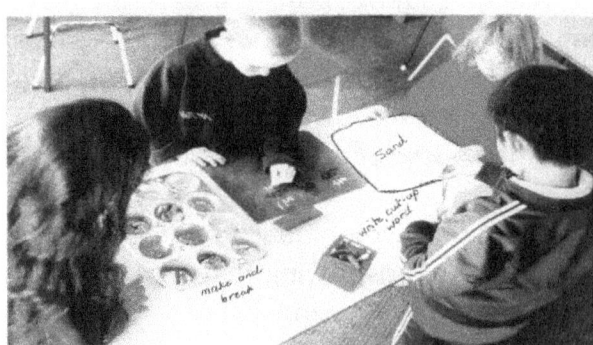

Practising new words			

	Whiteboard (or chalk board)		
Magnetic letters		Sand tray	Figure 8
	Makes and breaks		

Children at the 'After Guided Reading word centre'

Initially, plastic letters for the word only are placed on the table but as children become more knowing about what to do and more responsible about finishing the locations independently, all letters can be left in a departmentalized container and children source the wanted letters themselves.

Children **do not** use this learning centre as a general activity, instead it is used only after the Guided Reading discussion and showing of a strategy.

Children move from location to location quickly. They stand while they move around the locations. When all four practising locations have been finished children go to their first activity which is to re-read their Guided Reading book(s).

You could place a card with the word written on it in large letters and appropriate letters in a small plastic bag and children can access them during Independent Activities (this is a wonderful activity for older children with word problems).

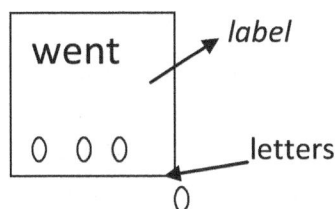

Focal point: **Recording vocabulary development**

Record on a 'Guided Reading Record' sheet each word the children has practised and other information.

Daily recording is important. Most teachers work with more than one group and to remember details you record, words learnt, what good strategies were used, what problems arose which you have either 'fixed up' in that session and will reinforce the next day or you will teach a strategy the next day at the beginning of the Guided Reading lesson.

Guided Reading – Early Readers (levels 1-9) [*Black line master 1, page 105]

Group				Recording Example
Before reading: *Knowing the story ... predicting (title, cover, text illustrations)* During reading: *Think about the story, listen to yourself read, modelling comprehension, 'fix-up' strategies* After reading: *Quick Retell, after approx L.6 Partner retell. Discussion – pre-planned open ended questions, show a strategy on a word. Go to 'After Guided Reading practise a word' centre*				
Date	L	Book title	Discussion focus Word strategy	Comment
	L E		*is* *the* *link* *in*	**MP (child's initials) not looking at pictures for cues** *During Shared Reading demonstrate how pictures help to predict some words. During Guided Reading, carefully 'read' the pictures – text/picture match*

If you want you can assess the retention of the word patterns children have learnt from the Guided Reading session. At the end of 3-4 weeks flash the words and children read the words, fluently. Then call each word and they write, fluently.

Learning to build an ever increasing number of high-frequency words can happen at other times as well:

- **Reading and singing** rhymes, chants, catchy poems, picture and big books.
  After the reading use a window device, or coloured highlighter tape and bring to the children's attention a particular high – frequency word to learn.

  Questions you ask, *What does the word begin with?*
  End with? What is the small word?

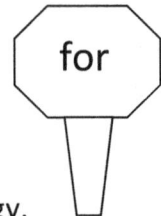

  for

  It is more effective clumping sounds than using a letter by letter strategy.

  Then you return to the text and read the word in context.

- **Interactive Writing** (information page 103) **and Shared Writing** are terrific for teaching word strategies. Children suggest an idea e.g. a sentence and they suggest spelling. In this environment the teacher demonstrates strategies to use when deciphering spelling words; further, he or she asks children to tell what strategy they used.

- **Classroom individual spelling programme** (see Liz Simon *Strategic Spelling, 2004*)

- Use **literature** to study words/phrases and their role in sentences, thus connecting words and grammar.

- Play **games** such as high-frequency word Bingo

- **Jigsaws** of rhymes, prefixes, suffixes/spelling patterns etc. | Un / health \ y |

- **Memory** games | cat | | cat |

- A special time (e.g. 10 minutes) for **'Word Wise'** is set aside each day to consolidate strategy use when decoding words; learning to choose the appropriate strategy or strategies for the word. Further, relating the 'Word Wise' word to grammatical constructions (noun groups, verb groups) helps children in their knowledge about language when reading.

Helpful Hint
An incidental, but important point: As children read in Guided Reading try not to interrupt the flow. It is more appropriate to note the few words a child cannot read, tell them the word and teach strategies after the reading.

10

Teachers say, "I find I am often in a quandary about grouping and re-grouping."

Teachers say, "I was told to take a Running Record on each child every week."

Chapter focal point

Flexible grouping

Diagnostic Assessment and flexible grouping
Diagnostic Assessment (keeping data)

In a classroom, varying grouping patterns is something that happens throughout the day. Teachers, during Shared Reading, Read Aloud, Shared Writing, gather the whole class to model - joint construction of texts, show models, deconstruct models (text structures, language structures and vocabulary, how to use digital technology, build field knowledge). Then they move into small groupings according to ability and needs, interests, assignments, (e.g. Guided Reading, Guided Writing, discussion groups, involvement in reinforcing activities or more challenging tasks e.g. inquiry, using internet/podcasts) and then individual learning (e.g. conferencing, blogs, wiki-spaces). This is one aspect of a balanced literacy programme.

Focal point: **Flexible grouping**

Flexible grouping is also 'part and parcel' within Guided Reading. Guided Reading is about differentiated teaching and learning with children progressing at different levels. Students' reading development is different for each student which necessitates the need to be flexible and ready at any time to alter group configurations.

Case Study #3

I have experienced some children in Guided Reading to be 'bubbling' along, steadily moving up levels and they come to a point and fluent reading may not be happening. Or some children struggle on all the levels because of something that is inhibiting their progress, for example, some children self-correct too much and this interferes with fluency. There are some children who are kept in the same group but there are signs that they should be challenged more.

When working with teachers, I became aware of the problem of how the choice of texts can make such a difference.

Although, reflecting on my days as a Reading Recovery teacher this was constantly a problem. The initial years were fraught with frustration because of the lack of reading material. The books could only be described as 'variable literature' which were scrounged from the school library or 'take home' books from the resource room; they were an assortment of texts from different series, some were picture books. What was discovered, that going from varied types of books did not enable the building of repeated high-frequency words. In addition, books that were considered 'easy' to read in the first pages, by page 7 became books that could be placed three to six levels higher than the original levelling. Sentence structures were difficult; they were not speech-like, they did not follow a literature pattern that children most likely were familiar with. I chose books because I thought they were interesting and motivating, but what I found was they were difficult and took away the pleasure of reading for the children. Then PM story books, a series developed by New Zealand educators, came to the rescue (see page 56).

Following on, small books began to be especially written and levelled for Guided Reading. Multiple connected texts make all the difference to children's early reading success. Why make it hard for children when they are learning to read?

And it was not always the texts fault! Children often progressed up the levels until Level 10 and there, some stumbled and I found that I had not secured these children's early strategy use – partly due to pushing all the children in the group into reading too hard texts, highlighting **all** the errors and not confirming good reading behaviour, for example, getting parts of the word correct or the word children have given making sense.

Focal point: **Diagnostic Assessment and flexible grouping**

The big question is **when** are children moved up or down levels and sometimes regrouped? This is a teacher judgement based on Diagnostic Assessment, in this case, Running Records and Miscue Analysis (for more information consult Marie M. Clay's *Running Records for classroom teachers* 2000).

Running Records are continually taken throughout the year to evaluate a child's reading development and identify the next teaching point; this ensures a student's continuous reading development. The information gained from these assessments also **identifies children's reading levels.** As readers are diagnostically assessed (Running Record/Miscue Analysis and don't forget **comprehension questions),** the teacher makes decisions about groups and regrouping.

Decisions are **also** being made as children read during each Guided Reading session. The teacher **records** children's strengths (e.g. strategies they are using, self-correcting when a piece does not make sense) and weaknesses (e.g. how often they are stopping at words) and the teaching point to work on and reinforce. These are brief recordings (see below example) and Running Records being ongoing, confirm your written observations.

Guided Reading – Developing Readers Group *approx Level 10 +*
Group

Before reading: *Knowing the story ... predicting (title, cover, text illustrations)*				
During reading: *Think about the story, listen to yourself read, modelling comprehension and 'fix-up' strategies* mainly ask "How can you help yourself?" "What strategy did you use...?"				
After reading: Partner retell, discussion -*pre-planned open ended questions, quick word strategy*				
Date	L	Book title	Discussion focus Word strategy	Comment
	10		**What was the problem?**	2/3 Run Rec **ST** (child's initials) read fluently, comprehending at this level, using predicting, connecting strategies throughout reading, discussion.
	10		**What was the solution?**	
	10			**LE–** leaving out words that distort meaning.
	11			Give cut up sentence work.

(Black line masters 2 (example), 5 (recording), pages 106 and 109).

A teacher is constantly observing and is not only prepared to regroup children, but to find the cause of the problem and to make decisions about what texts should be used. Embedding assessment into the small group reading session and giving immediate feedback will lead to continuous self-improvement and the development of positive attitudes towards reading.

Helpful Hints
Teachers are often concerned about having varied levels in one group and it is important to have the most suitable reading texts to support readers at each of those levels.   • If one group has been assessed as having readers reading at levels 10, 11, 12 they take the approach of choosing books at level 11. Or they may choose books where students at different levels have a common need, so they choose level 10. The main thought in a teacher's mind is that the group has a similar level of control of the reading process and that the level range is not too wide (essential for early and developing readers).   • Teachers who have one child at a very low level, say, in grade 2, try to collaborate with another teacher having the same grade (or grade 1) and they divide the groups among each other. This approach gives more group options.   *Note:* An argument against this is that the classroom teacher needs to know what each child in his or her classroom is achieving; there are many scenarios of literacy learning in the classroom which require the teacher to know about and react to all the literacy learners in the class. So this is a complicated issue.

Focal point: **Diagnostic Assessment**

Running Records and Miscue Analysis.

There is an easy, viable organizational procedure to put in place for the taking of Running Records in the classroom.

Running Records/ Miscue Analyses in the classroom

The day you decide to schedule assessments (Running Records) you do so with **one** child from each Guided Reading group. Over a month you should have completed Running records on all the children in your class.

The particular group is sitting at the Guided Reading area as you take the Running Record on the child.

You continue Guided Reading with each group (approximately three) **after** the Running Record is completed.

A child's reading behaviour (Running Record) is assessed as she/he reads aloud an **unfamiliar book.**

The child being assessed (Running Record) moves to one side and will read independently. The **child reads approximately 100-150 words**. As this is happening the rest of the group are re-reading books from previous Guided Reading sessions.

The group reforms and **all children read the new book** introduced for the Running Record. A discussion follows. You may want to keep the assessed child for a few minutes after the Guided Reading session to show a needed problem solving strategy.

Taking the Running Record Procedure:
- Sit the child alongside you. You face one direction, the child the opposite direction (love seat). You can easily see the book as the child reads. Or just sit the child next to you.
- The child reads an unfamiliar book, at the current instructional level.
- The teacher supplies the book title and gives the book for the child to explore; the child interprets the pictures unaided and takes note of the layout of the text.
- The child does own orientation (the purpose being, knowing whether he can orientate himself to the story).
- The teacher takes the Running Record giving no prompts but supplies difficult words after a reasonable pause by the child. Make additional notes on fluency and expressiveness.

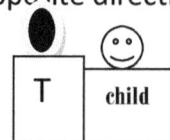

Miscue Analysis:

- The Analysis is done in your own time.
- Calculate the accuracy rate (95% -98%).
- Examine the Running Record to find out what strategies the child is using when making unsuccessful attempts and self-corrections. Analysing the running record will tell you whether the reader is over-reliant on one strategy. For example, he or she concentrates on decoding and does not check meaning or he or she concentrates on meaning and syntax and forgets to confirm by referring to print detail (*See:* M.M. Clay. 2007. *An Observation Survey...* for details on taking and analysing Running Records).
- The child retells (maybe to the rest of his group) or you ask comprehension questions or you chat about understandings. Recording how the child is comprehending covers four comprehension developments:

    - recalls information (RI)
    - makes inferences (MI)
    - determines important ideas (DI)
    - synthesizes information (SI)

Running Records/comprehension assessment will help you track movement of groups, for example, placing a child in a new grouping because abilities and needs have changed. A group may move to a new level weekly. A group remaining at the same level for more than two weeks requires a teacher to assess the guiding role she/he is performing.

Note: Asking comprehension questions is sufficient assessment for levels 20+.

For children on Reading Recovery it is wonderful (essential) if the same teaching strategies are reinforced in the classroom.

Data is always kept. When I was working in USA my husband created this data collection form (Excel) for Guided Reading which monitored the movement of children up the levels (Figure 9). Make a similar form for each classroom or better still have it networked into each classroom.

Continuous Monitoring of reading levels K-3																with each assessment date the box												
Running Record & comprehension retell and questions. Remembering flexible grouping.																								Comprehension Qs only				
Guided Reading	1	2	3	4	5	6	7	8	9	10	11	12	13	14	15	16	17	18	19	20	21	22	23	24	25	26	27	28	29
Children's Names by Groups																												

Figure 9

11

"I thought I had to begin Guided Reading straight away with my Reception children."

Chapter focal points
Early days at school
Developing letter, symbol knowledge

Children do not partake in Guided Reading lessons until they know at least 75% of the alphabet. The reason for this is that the first visual strategy you direct children to is, "*What does the word begin with.*"

Controlling left-to right movement and return sweep, connecting graph-o-phonic information with phonemic awareness, noticing and interpreting details in pictures, awareness of reading making sense, paying close attention to print, matching words one-on-one and comprehension strategies can all be taught during Guided Reading.

Focal point: **Early days at school**

During the early days at school the literacy learning experiences are **Shared Reading, Reading Aloud, Interactive Writing and Independent Reading**. The emphasis with new children is listening to the reading of prose (Big Books), chants, rhymes (posters) and picture books until they are ready to read independently in Guided Reading.

Some children may be new to language patterns, for example, rhyming patterns, thinking about and sequencing stories while other children will have prior knowledge of early reading behaviour. Some children may not have developed phonemic awareness, may not be confident speakers, while other children have begun to match sounds to symbols and are assured speakers. Whatever, all children at this early stage in their schooling love stories read in an interesting and dramatic manner. They respond by reading repetitive parts and in this environment children join in reading when they are ready; they are visualizing the wonderful ideas presented in the stories and you are concentrating on comprehension strategies such as predicting, making connections and retelling and they interpret stories.

Independent Reading

During Independent Reading time, children new to school are not required to be readers as such, but handle books and re-read books teachers have read to them and create stories as they make a connection with the picture and what they know about the story and story language. It is so thrilling to hear a child interpreting stories that have been read to them, for example, after listening to many readings of 'The Three Billy Goats Gruff' a child's reading was expressed, "There was a horrible, horrible Troll hiding under the bridge, along came a little goat. Poor little goat wasn't allowed to cross the bridge. The Troll shouted, "Who is that on my bridge?" and the beautifully sequenced narration continued. During Independent Reading time they put into practise what they are learning during Shared Reading and Reading Aloud and of course, connecting what they have learnt at home.

Focal point: **Developing letter, symbol knowledge**

As well as Shared Reading, Reading Aloud, Interactive writing and Independent Reading, children are involved in a concentrated programme where they learn letters quickly. Learn a letter each week, to recognize and write.

Begin by testing the letter knowledge of children (see Liz Simon's *Strategic Spelling*, 2004). When you have the information from the assessment, you have choices:

  - choose a letter to work on that **most** children cannot recognize/write:
  - choose letters of a child or children who has the **least unknown** letters. (You may have this child/children move into Guided Reading quickly);
  - If children writing capitals, choose to learn the matching lower case letters. (These children may also move into Guided Reading quickly).

Activities to assist children develop letter knowledge (see Liz Simon's *Strategic Spelling, 2004*).

  I.   Read/sing the abc song, *'now I know my ABC'*
  II.   Read small letter books (PM Alphabet Starters (1995) or Alphakids (1998)
  III.   Write the letter on white or chalk boards in front of you
  IV.   Interactive writing (see page 103). Begin by writing a simple sentence, later move to compound sentences adding *'and'*. It is good to begin with *I am [name.]* You can later write other phrases: *I can…., I can see……, I went ……, I like…….* You can repeat each of these for a week.

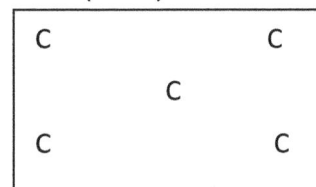

c		c
	c	
c		c

After, writing these initial phrases, you move to general news/ideas from the children.

Write the Interactive written sentence on a sentence strip, the strip can be cut up and placed into packages for children to re-read. Or you write the child's own writing attempts on a sentence strip for them to take home and read. You select about 4 different children each day to do this.

Some extra activities can be:

- Making alphabet books.

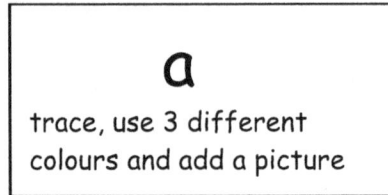

a
trace, use 3 different colours and add a picture

Children can practise the letter by using different coloured crayons and tracing over the letter. Glue pictures with items beginning with the letter.

- Computer letter/word games. Select games/tasks that have a precise purpose.

- Making little books.

Help the children to write the phrases you have been doing in Interactive writing. Ask them questions e.g. *what does ..... begin with?* Encourage the children to write the first letter, you can write the rest.

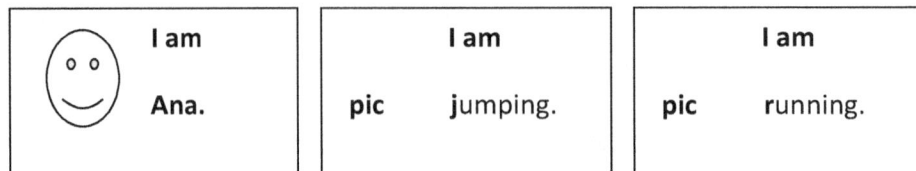

I am Ana.	I am pic jumping.	I am pic running.

12

Chapter focal points

Complexity of texts

Guided Reading for older students

Multiple learning focuses

Varied Guided Reading approaches
  Typical Guided Reading session when using non-fiction texts
  Atypical Guided Reading session when using non-fiction texts
  Interactive Shared Reading for small groups
  Reciprocal Teaching

Discussion groups

Journals

*"In primary grades children are learning to read
and in upper grades they are reading to learn."*
Is this true?

The person who coined this phrase may have done a disservice to older readers. The view is that once children learn to read and comprehend in the primary years they are able to easily cope with any type of reading.

In the early years, teaching and learning to read is rather 'compact'; familiar narrative texts and if non-fiction it is a narrative form. In the higher years teaching and learning to read is more diverse. Older students go from one type of reading to another, for example, they not only skim read texts but they are also required to read deeply. They read on-screen as well as print. On-screen reading may demand more than reading print, navigating different pathways while at the same time closely focusing on the material that is being read.

With increased curriculum demands and the expectation of independence, teachers may think differently about older students. Teachers may overestimate older students' comprehension development with the expectation that students have learnt to read in grades reception to two; a change in teaching practices result. As a colleague of mine once related to me, students from approximately grade 3 onwards are *'assigned and assessed'*. That is, a teacher may tell the students the task outline without support of any kind e.g. models shown and deconstructed and talked about.

Just when children begin to move beyond decoding words and seem to gain control over meaning, they are now expected to read content laden, complex texts independently and with complete understanding and, furthermore, transform what has been read into assignments.

Focal point: **Complexity of texts**

For older students there is a change in the type and complexity of texts they are reading. Even with **novels** older students may find that they are more convoluted and sophisticated; meaning can be lost because they,

- are reading longer books and chapters; they may read a story for a longer period of time;

- are comprehending longer more complex story lines;

- need to reflect upon unfamiliar events and experiences;

- are reading a variety of writing styles. One author may introduce the characters on the first page, whilst another author may write in a more obscure way and introduce the problem and it is not until chapter two the main character is introduced. Some authors do not state the character who is uttering dialogue, therefore the reader has to read closely and infer who the speaker is.

Older students are expected to 'read to learn'. Reading and understanding **information** and **expository texts** and **transforming** the **information** into **summaries, presentations, assignments,** are part of the classroom scene. Cynthia Shanahan (2008) points out that many students have difficulty reading content-area texts when involved in inquiry and research. These difficulties arise because,

- of general reading difficulties;

- students are learning English;

- students lack appropriate background knowledge, skills and strategies.

Older students reading exposition texts and textbooks, often have to make sense of **abstract** subject matter often far removed from their personal experience. The 'abstract, de-contextualized nature of the language, fails to provide explanation of technical vocabulary, fails to provide general explanations or examples' (Cynthia Shanahan (2008). Older readers are dealing with more complex sentence structures where grammatical types like,

- noun groups (*a group of <u>words</u>* - nouns, articles, adjectives and conjunctions are contained in one clause);

- extended clause/clauses are repackaged into a noun group condensing ideas, describing a single topic or event;

- noun forms of verbs (nominalization) changes an action into a concept (an abstract thing). The intention of nominalization is to make writing, especially the writing of non-fiction texts, more impersonal and precise e.g. 'The people who first came to Australia...' is made more succinct, 'Early settlers...'

- embedded clauses which interrupt the clause, 'The woods, which are dark at this time of day, made Jesse shiver;

- negative statements, 'He <u>has</u> <u>nothing</u> in his bag';

- similes, figurative language and metaphors can confuse readers.

Because of the increase in specialized vocabulary, non-fiction texts are more difficult to read. *This is unlike every-day spoken language that children in the early primary years are used to reading; their types of texts have more clauses and less content words – more like spoken language.*

Focal point: **Guided Reading for older students**

Note: If there is the same new learning for all in the class you teach the whole class. It may be the case, though, that a few students are not able to apply the learning and need more personalized exposure, so small group instruction is implemented.

Guided Reading is implemented in Upper Primary (and Secondary); the aim is the same as Guided Reading for younger children:

- Differentiating learning (catering for all learning needs).

- Giving children strategies and practise to read independently more sophisticated texts.

- Inculcating critical thinking processes.

In addition, older readers:

- Use their reading to complete assignments independently; discuss issues, ask their own questions to construct meaning.

Throughout a child's learning at school the cognitive (and social) demands of literacy is continually evolving and diversifying. Literacy learning becomes more complex and refined. As students are experiencing new contexts they will want to know the relevance of the learning and how to connect and apply understandings and skills.

Even in upper grades students are *'learning to read'* varied and more sophisticated texts. The upper grade teacher is prepared to implement small group meetings to cater for the needs of his or her students.

Guided Reading for older students has different emphases than the 'regular' Guided Reading for young readers:

- Grouping does not depend on levels but rather students are grouped depending on **similar learning needs** (e.g. unpacking of dense material, understanding complex sentence structures) and **interests** and **topics being studied**. These groupings are even more flexible than early, developing and early fluent groupings.

- A wide variety of more complex material is read, e.g. extracts from information texts (including digital), articles, narratives.

- Older students read to gather information to transform into another form.

- There are multiple learning focuses (discussed further on).

- There are varied Guided Reading scenarios (discussed further on).

- Assessment, *formative* (similar to diagnostic) is ongoing and qualitative feedback is forwarded as students are reading and completing tasks. Formative assessment is undertaken during reading and writing conferences and responding to journal entries (e.g. blogs and wikispaces) as well as criteria-based observation of oral performances.

Focal point: **Multiple learning focuses**

Small group learning reflects whole class learning. When a problem situation arises or a particular interest is shown, or some students need to be challenged further, a teacher of older students knows, the importance of the personal, small group learning.

Case Study #5

A teacher working with small groups in the classroom has group (**A**) sitting with her and is introducing a more complex text (a digital text) and she shares strategies, for example, choosing material by having more specific information to look for and using the guide *Readability, Usefulness, Trustworthiness,* (Baildon & Baildon, 2008) (explanation see page 104).

After spending 15 minutes with this group, another group (**B**) sits with the teacher to explore several texts of narrative genre being studied by the class e.g. mystery, science fiction.

Small groups at different times may be introduced to,

- strategies e.g. unpacking precise sentences into 'meaning units' e.g. "the author has written *'the settlement'* (noun group), this means where the settlers have gathered";

- a way of enhancing their comprehension strategies when reading more complex texts (learning grammatical features, questions, visualizing, inferring, main points and synthesizing all the elements);

- how to deconstruct the language of particular texts, e.g. language of influence such as in historical material, articles, newspapers. Reading alone students may not be able to discern bias and you show them how to analyse evidence;

- the behaviour needed to have self-reflective discussions about literacy;

- the specific skill or text elements (dialogue, nonfiction captions, use of literary devices etc);

- ways of sustaining comprehension over time;

- knowledge of sentence structure (clauses, sub-clauses) that help understanding allowing the reader to anticipate future events;

- a different type of reading - skimming and scanning to quickly access relevant information to answer an inquiry question - the ability to scan or skim an information book is essential. This is different from the type of reading of the whole text they have been used to; they are selective, reading only headings and the themes (topic sentences) and key words, all the time keeping a question to be answered in their minds;

- critical interpretations of the theme, how an author's bias is revealed in his writing and presentation; how a period in history may determine future happenings.

Focal point: **Varied Guided Reading approaches**

Typical Guided Reading session when using non-fiction texts:

Before reading:

- Ask the students to tell what they know about the topic
- Have a white board or a chart to record a question from each student in the group – something they would like to learn about the topic
- If there is a 'contents', look at the contents and read the technical language and meanings in the glossary and see if they think their questions will be answered by reading the book they have in their hand
- (Ask students to recall the information they read the day before)

During Reading:

- Map the student's reading (they may read it over a 2-3 day period)
  (More questions may be added to the list.)

At the end of the reading of the text:

- Discuss "*Were your questions answered*?"
- To begin the discussion, ask an open ended question that relates to the reading, for example:
  - *Is it important [that monkeys and apes live on earth]?* or
  - *What would the earth be like if we didn't have ....?* or
  - *How would it effect people if ....?*

This will lead to a critical discussion where students evaluate what they have read, make judgments, give opinions based on what they have learnt from the text.

Atypical Guided Reading session when using non-fiction texts

Case Study #6

A teacher of grade 4/5 and I were working with a group of readers who showed an interest in robots. The classroom topic was 'Japan' and to give the topic vivacity she searched Google to see what information was available about robots. A terrific article was found and a copy given to each member of the group.

Included in the Guided Reading session was a quick podcast viewing of the 'cleverness' of the robot. At the end of the article there were further sites about robots to access and better still, comments from viewers and a facility for students to make comments of their own (both tasks she directed the group to complete during Independent Task time while she worked with another Guided Reading Group).

So from the hard copy readers held in their hands and a viewing on the computer they return to the computer and keep researching... and write reviews to share.

Using the article the teacher began by orienting the readers to the piece. She showed the headline only and students revealed their knowledge about robots and predicted what the information may be about. Her teaching focus for this group was predicting word meanings using context clues. She had previously observed that this small group of students was not utilizing the strategy when reading.

She asked the group, "What do you think *dexterity* means? Read the sentence beginning *manual dexterity*..." students read, 'manual dexterity capable of picking up a drinking straw'. They surmised the meaning; she pointed out that the strategy of reading ahead helps to define meanings of unfamiliar words. She continued with two other examples. The teacher stressed the point that good readers search the context to 'guess' the meaning of unknown words. The students wrote on post-its, their meanings and were told that after the group meeting they check meanings in the dictionary. This Guided Reading focus would be repeated in future sessions with this group.

For the discussion she posed this question, 'Do you think this article is well written?' She wanted the group to form points of view about the quality of the article, e.g. the ideas, the language.

Interactive Shared Reading for small groups

Case Study #7

A pre-service teacher in my tutorial class at Flinders University, (Adelaide, South Australia), in reply to an article set for study about classroom students struggling to read and understand material they are expected to digest to complete assignments, made the written comment:

Many older students in schools that I have worked with (as a School Service Officer) find various texts complicated. As a result this can lead to a lack of motivation causing some students to give up and not pursue the task. I have worked with an assortment of students with literacy difficulties. I regularly see this predicament of not comprehending instructions and materials given to them ... need to break down the texts for struggling readers.

Students who find reading difficult quickly lose the will to participate. It is a perplexing problem which is often solved by teachers giving these readers 'easier' texts to read. Often these texts are not connected to classroom learning and certainly they do not advance student's ability to read more complex texts.

Consider this alternative approach where delayed readers read more complex texts with teacher support.

Interactive Shared Reading is a small group of older readers reading enlarged print along with the teacher. The teacher guides them as they read.

Cynthia Shanahan (2008) advocates that, 'with high level of instructional support, students who are delayed in their reading may be able to read [more complex text] when they **read with support'**. That support would be 'providing background information, 'unpacking' complex language into spoken-language, explaining meaning associated with vocabulary and strategy instruction ['*Think about...*'] to improve students' ability to learn from even very difficult text'.

Case Study #8

During 'inquiry and research' workshops that I give, I suggest that teachers not only implement Interactive Shared Reading (deconstructing text) with the class but also small groups of delayed readers. Having students in interactive small group meetings where the teacher takes a major role reading the text, lessens the anxiety often felt by struggling readers and keeps these students exposed to complex texts, learning far more than they would, reading simplified, shortened pieces independently.

With the advent of interactive whiteboards intentional instruction of complex ideas and vocabulary can be achieved by scanning and displaying extracts on the board. During Interactive Shared Reading you lead the reading and you and the students **talk** about choices, connections, examples and anything else that assists students to read independently. A teacher's aim is to move older students' learning into the realm of their control; the teacher relates strategies and ideas that help students understand texts and motivate the desire to read.

Case Study #9

During a science lesson, the teacher takes a small group of delayed readers to one side to read and deconstruct a complex piece. He knows that **nominalization** is essential learning for students reading scientific information texts. It involves replacing verbs (or adjectives, adverbs) with noun phrases, usually by affixing a morpheme for example, the verb 'oxidize' to the noun 'oxidant'; the meaning of words are subject specific, the writing is more abstract and precise.

> Text: Water and oxygen in the air oxidize iron to form rust. Oxidation happens when an oxidant such as oxygen and other different substances come into contact.

Teacher thinking aloud: *When I read this I form a picture in my head. I see a bike made of iron and it is left in the rain and I know air - oxygen is all around. Over time this combination of oxygen and water **oxidizes** (verb) the metal in the bike, the iron turns to rust.*
Student thinking aloud: *What, so the oxygen and air **oxidizes** the iron in the bike and makes it rusty?*

Teacher confirms the student's thinking and continues his thinking aloud: *The author then expands further on the explanation and this time uses the noun **'oxidation'**. Instead of the author saying 'rust' she uses the noun 'oxidation' making the information more precise and subject-specific.*

After reactions from students, the teacher explains further *...when iron reacts with the* **oxidant** (noun) *oxygen in the air, this combination of one substance with another substance causes rust to form.* He stops and some thinking aloud from his students happens.

An additional pointer for his students*:*

When you read science texts authors change similar meaning words from verbs into nouns to expand the information and the reader's understanding. Now let's read this piece together.

Learning to read for information is **question driven**; it requires questions to be asked and answered.

Case study #10

While the class is involved in reading and responding to questions, the teacher sits at a table with a small group of delayed readers and displays a question,

Share a few aspects about the role of the early Pharaohs. Did they shape the identity of Egyptian society, for the ruling elite, artisans and peasants?

The many clauses in this question are deconstructed and the teacher explains meanings. The teacher may show how a student takes the question apart and determines what should be noticed; how to read closely and the importance of re-reading the question and inferring meanings of words by reading ahead.

For delayed readers learning **grammatical features** and rehearsing sentence structures (syntax) assists the fluency of their reading and their understanding of the text:

- **Themes** (topic sentences) being announced at the beginning of a paragraph foreshadow the content of the reading piece. Noun groups, prepositional phrases (*In addition,*) and adverbs (*Furthermore, Suddenly*) are paragraph openers.
- **Cohesive devices,** repetitions, word groupings *colonize, colonialism, colony, colonist,* noun/pronoun connections (*Mary... she*), text connectives 'and', 'but'.
- **Passive voice** either depersonalizes writing, 'The disagreement <u>was initiated</u>...' OR adds suspense (instead of, *the lion crept up on its prey (active voice)* the passive *the zebra <u>was spooked</u> by something approaching from behind.*

During Interactive Shared Reading with small groups the teacher may,

- generate a wide range of possible meanings and interpretations; different slants;
- explore themes (stories, issues), comparing differences/sameness;
- infer... because this was said/happened, this could mean ...;
- view how the texts are crafted;
- use decoding strategies ('fix-up' strategies) on technical or unusual words (see chapter 3 page 26);
- verbally structure a summary a paragraph at a time by noting the theme and locating key words.

Reciprocal Teaching

Another small group meeting scenario that relates to non-fiction texts but involves a higher level of student independence than Guided Reading is **Reciprocal Teaching** (Palinscar and Brown, 1986). This group reading and resultant discussion can be implemented when students are involved in inquiry/research. Each reader has a copy of a particular short section of a **complex** text (**mainly non-fiction**); the text is purposely selected by the teacher and the piece is independently read by each member of the group and then discussed in a framework defined by four comprehension strategies –

◊ predicting/inferring
◊ clarifying
◊ generating questions
◊ summarizing   (child recording sheet Black line master 15, page 119).

The student leader of the group guides his (or her) peers to talk and think their way through a text. The students are learning from each other and building their understandings through discussion.

Initially, the teacher will guide students through the learning of each strategy and then shift the responsibility of integrating the independent use of them to the students. Teachers take less of an instructional role than they do in Guided Reading. After observing a session teachers may give feedback of how to improve, say, the strategy, summarizing.

There are two rotating discussion roles – leader and summarizer.

The procedure:
The teacher schedules the gathering of the group.

After reading the title, headings or the first passage, the group **leader** begins by asking members of the group to predict the likely content. Connections between the topic and prior knowledge are made (the teacher may also have input at this stage).

The group goes to a quiet area in the classroom where they write their **predictions,** independently read the piece and record any **inferences** and plan thought provoking **questions.**

All members write a summary with one member of the group being designated the role of the **summarizer** and this member will, at the end of the discussion, tell the main ideas in the piece of reading; showing the purpose of the text. Other members may join in and add to the summary or say (in a nice way) parts that they think are unnecessary (giving reasons why they think as they do).

To maintain meaning and build understanding all members of the group may isolate ideas, vocabulary, terminology, concepts or a strategy to be **clarified**; they may prepare questions as they read or ask for clarification of a member's contribution during the discussion.

All the time the group **leader** is spontaneously encouraging participation helping the group discussion to proceed, perhaps extend ideas or model a possible response and justification of an idea. In other words the leader takes the role of the teacher.

Reciprocal teaching gives students strategies and an organization of thinking they use when reading non-fiction independently and in discussing texts with others; they develop the ability to question and think critically about texts. Reciprocal teaching allows students to evaluate and offer opinions and justifications based on their reading of the current text.
Moving from Guided Reading to Reciprocal Teaching (and Book Clubs, see Liz Simon's *Thinkers and Performers Bringing Critical Thinking Alive, 2010*) provides a continuum of developmental reading experiences.

Focal point: **Discussion groups**

The emphasis with older students is more involvement in **small discussion groups**; discussing their thinking, evaluating their learning and their progress. They may read web sites and discuss their findings or a newspaper article and discuss their opinions, all the time referring to evidence presented in the text or other texts they have read.

Independent discussion groups happen in Guided Reading and Reciprocal Teaching (partner talk can also happen during or after Read Aloud). Discussion is all about children reflecting on questions asked, thinking critically about what they have read, applying their knowledge, drawing conclusions and forming and sharing and justifying their opinions.

Discussion groups, of course, are a type of compelling debate where students respond to their reading; they think, talk and reach understandings, say, about subject matter they are studying, that they may not reach alone.

The least the teacher intrudes **during** group discussion the more the group confidently talk to each other. The teacher's role is to give feedback after discussion where ideas and strategies are forwarded.

The degree that you allow student-independence, as regards groups arranging their own agenda, will depend on the cooperative skills they have developed. There are expectations relating to behaviour and relationships between students that need to be considered (see Liz Simon's *Thinkers and Performers Bringing Critical Thinking Alive, chapter 2.* 2010).

Focal point: **Journals**

An aspect closely associated with older readers is journals (handwritten or on-screen).

After a book is introduced to students during a Guided Reading session and after the students have independently read the book (or article or non-fiction piece), children write handwritten journal entries (cover Black line master 16, page 120) or on-screen Microsoft Word, blogs, or similar, noting questions, their impressions, clarifications, ideas and reflections. Journals contain drawings, graphs and short written responses.

The **journal** or **diary** can be the prompt for a particular focus for small discussion groups. Journal entries may reveal student misunderstandings or difficulties with a concept.

All literacy experiences are recorded in literacy journals e.g. research notes may be recorded, graphic organizers for planning, connections between books, meaning in books, author's words, what was learned about literacy, elements of language, responding to books, supportive features readers have found. Students continually refer to it and teachers can refer to it at times or if it is an on-screen journal they can reply to children's entries.

The great advantage of a class blog is that the author of the blog, either a student or teacher, begins by making a comment about a recent book read and their peers (audience), reply with the original respondent reacting to their opinions, ideas. This type of discussion can be ongoing. Of course, protocols are established by the teacher with responses and models of appropriate language being established.

The school or organization generally determines the software to be used in the school, for example, 2Publish/21Cla.

13

Chapter focal point

Planning for Guided Reading

Book Choice

Case study #12

Ask yourself, if you had not read the book beforehand,

How would you choose a book that is within the control of a particular reading group while allowing for some learning opportunities? How would you interact with a Guided Reading group if you have not pre-read the book they are reading? How do you plan the introduction, ask the right questions? How would you choose a focus? How would you give appropriate feedback to help children improve their reading and thinking? How would you find out if the book was suitable for a particular group?

To illustrate the importance of careful choice and prereading material in relation to a particular group; e.g children from language backgrounds other than English typify somewhat a quarter of our school population. From the author Pauline Gibbon's 1993 book *Learning to learn in a second language,* the classroom literacy program is certain to be a major resource for language development for bi-lingual children. A perceptive and knowledgeable teacher takes into account the fact that these children are not only learning a new language, but that they are learning in that new language as well. Teachers choosing books know their students' culture, interests, understandings, skills. If the topic and vocabulary are unfamiliar, it is common for bilingual children to ,

- read slowly;
- have poor comprehension;
- be unable to predict, draw conclusions and self correct.

A teacher's preparations prior to meeting with any Guided Reading group supports students' equitable access to successful reading.

Focal point: **Planning for Guided Reading**

Teachers choose suitable texts and while pre-reading the texts foreshadow obscurities that could arise. They plan how to eliminate blocks to fluent reading and understanding. Teachers pre-read texts to decide whether children can relate to the topic, know the language structures and other relevant aspects. She plans comments to excite readers about the new text and prepares open-ended questions for discussion. She considers that even though a book is written especially for a level it may not 'grab' the reader. Furthermore, a continuum from easier to more complex texts can present problems. One book may have many levels within it.

Guided Reading, especially for early, developing and early fluent readers, is generally day by day planning (rather than week by week planning) with the teacher carefully mapping for the next day based on what was learnt from the previous day. What happens on day 1 becomes the focus day 2, whether it is teaching something new or reinforcing good strategies used and ideas presented. This more explicit planning happens when working with small groups and individuals.

Case Study #13

An observed teacher introducing the book 'Seed Folk' by Paul Fleishman knew the story well and was able to lead the group into making connections to the topic, 'Migration', being studied in the classroom; the organization of the story – chapters delineate each character telling their own story. She balances information with asking pertinent questions, for example, she tells them that each character's voice is the way the author created the story; she asks the group about the significance of the plants pictured on the cover; she checks on some vocabulary making sure the children know meanings before they read. She could not have done an in-depth introduction without reading the book beforehand and writing plans to guide the Guided Reading introduction.

Focal point: **Book Choice**

A teacher's choice of books is influenced by the supports books contain (including how the content relates to the readers) and whether the books match/support their readers' 'next learning'.

For early and developing readers teachers consider:

- The way sentences are structured – sentence patterns, word order, tenses, phrasing, return sweep, size of print;
- Where high frequency words are placed at the beginning, middle, and ending of sentences;
- Whether there is a problem and solution – so children can easily anticipate and predict;

- Whether when reading new books high-frequency words gradually increase;
- Whether pictures complement the text;
- Whether the same characters appear in the books so children know names, or can anticipate similar characteristics/experiences;
- Whether the content and accompanying vocabulary of a non-fiction text are familiar.

For early fluent readers

Both students and teachers are more discerning about the choice of reading material at this stage. Texts will be chosen for enjoyment as well as instruction and information gathering. Students will be reading a mixture of imaginative texts (novels, short stories, poems and plays), informative and persuasive texts (explanations and descriptions of natural phenomena, recounts of events, news bulletins, articles) (Australian Curriculum and Reporting Authority (ACARA 2012). Attention is still paid to children being able to read most of the material with some challenges that, with teacher input, help them advance. The widening of choice necessitates careful perusal of texts considering the purpose, interest and readability.

Teachers judge the suitability of the first novels, for example a teacher considers characteristics that are most likely to support readers new to reading novels (figures 10 and 11).

Not only are aspects of the first novel taken into account, but prompting comprehension strategies, moving from chapter to chapter and remembering what has been read would leave a teacher who has not read the books to be a silent participant.

Criteria for A level first novels

Language	Layout	Content
Simple vocabulary	Well spaced	Easy to follow sequence of events
Frequent use of many high frequency words and familiar words	Frequent illustrations matched to meaning at word and /or sentence level	Simple beginning, middle, end story structure
Short meaning contained sentences	Well defined paragraphs, often separated by pictures	One or two main characters, simply represented
Mainly natural language with some book language appearing	Chapter structure may be introduced to group ideas	Simple concepts, supported by illustrations
	Large to medium-sized print	Problem and solution
		Main ideas linked – simple and few

Figure 10

Criteria for B level first novels

Language	Layout	Content
Mainly natural language with some book language appearing	Illustrations that support main ideas at paragraph level or in surrounding text	Simple story structure of increasing length with beginning, middle, end defined
Mainly simple vocabulary, less repetitive	Well spaced, medium-sized print	Several ideas linked, to make up the story
Mixture simple sentences, and compound sentences	Direct speech frequently separated from other text	Familiar subject or strong support through illustrations
	Two or three short, related sentences in one paragraph	More than 1 problem more than 1 solution, then a final resolution
	May have short chapters to link ideas contained in paragraphs	Several main characters begin to be developed, other supporting characters appearing
	Clear paragraph breaks	

Figure 11

14

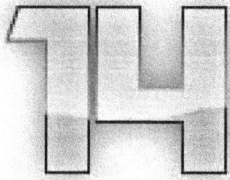

> *"I thought they read the same book for a week."*

Chapter focal point

Balancing reading and critical discussion

Focal point: **Balancing reading and critical discussion**

In Guided Reading young children reading small books, read a new fiction (or non-fiction) book every day/session. In the higher levels (e.g. levels 16+) where books have more print and in order to meet the balance of reading and critical discussion, these may be read in 15 or 20 minute sessions, over a 2 day period.

How long a book is read depends on the chosen text and what the teacher wishes to focus on.

Case Study #14

Introducing an information text about time (*It's about time*) (from Orbit collections 2001), there are only two chapters that are non-fiction, one an explanation and the other a report. The teacher may have chosen this text for the early fluent group because the particular group is studying 'time' in class or, she wants to compare the genres 'explanation' and 'report'. These chapters are read and discussed in two days

Day 1: The introduction: the group looks at the front cover and contents, *Is this text fiction or non-fiction? The contents list various genres, what does this mean? What are the non-fiction genres? What shall we read first, an explanation about daylight saving or the report 'Measuring Time over time'?*

Note: Non-fiction books, unlike fiction books, do not have to be read from front to back.

The children choose 'daylight saving' and the teacher lists questions the group would like to ask about daylight saving (not too many), e.g. *Does it mean there is less time in the day? What happens in those countries near the Arctic Circle where they have long times of daylight and long times of darkness? Do people like having daylight saving?*

The pictures are examined on the first page of this chapter to see if the children's questions can be answered e.g. a huge tick crosses sporting goods, a huge cross is placed over electrical goods. *What might this mean*? They read the diagram together and the teacher gives some information about the two identities mentioned in the explanation, Benjamin Franklin and William Willett. The children read silently in a selected area in the classroom and re-gather to discuss whether their questions have been answered. (If not, after Guided Reading, they could explore further information on Google).

Day 2: They read the report, questions may be added to the list. They read the information silently and after reading they re-gather and the teacher begins the discussion by asking, *What was this chapter mainly about? Can you tell me more? Remember what we talked about yesterday. Does this information relate to daylight saving? Have you noticed something more?*

The reading and discussion of these two chapters have fulfilled its purpose. The teacher will introduce a new book for the next Guided Reading session.

Another information text may have more interrelated chapters and the varied chapters may be read 3-4 days (including the follow-on discussion(s)).

Another example may be a story which raises many issues.

Case Study #15

Early Fluent readers read a short legend one day and the following 2-3 days discuss aspects of the tale.

The legend *Deirdre of the Sorrows* (Lock, Kely & Stafford,1995) is a tragic tale and is part of a much longer story known as the Ulster Cycle from ancient Ireland.

This tale is about the beautiful Deirdre and of her love for a handsome young warrior, who takes her away from the castle, and of a king's love for her. It has a dramatic ending where the king re-captures Deirdre and sets fire to buildings where Deirdre's husband and two brothers are sleeping. The roof lead melts and the hot lead drops into the brother's eyes and being unable to see who they are fighting, the two brothers kill each other. Deirdre's husband, on hearing of his brothers' demise kills himself. To escape marrying the king Deirdre 'plunges into the fast flowing water' of a river.

The Guided Reading procedure of an orientation to the story is conducted and children read the tale independently. There are many issues in this tale to discuss in depth in a Guided Reading environment:

- The relevance of prophesies? *Do you think what was prophesised needed to happen? What could be the turning point for the prophecy not to be fulfilled? Are there times the direction of people's destiny could have altered? What is the importance of prophesies and fates of the characters? Was the outcome to be expected?*

- The passive nature of the female role in that era. *Were Deidre's point of view, wishes considered?*

- The importance of beauty. *Is it necessary to have the two main characters, Deirdre and Naisi, described as beautiful? Two people were infatuated with Deirdre's beauty. Is beauty the only human feature that relationships are based on?*

- *What is each character's roles and relationship? Is this story about love?*

- Values of ancient times compared to now.

- The language, the commands that the author has the character's using. *Who uses commands in this story? Why do they talk that way?*

15

Chapter focal point

Reading material to begin Guided Reading in the school

Difficulties associated with levelling books

Focal point: **Reading material to begin Guided Reading in the school**

Lack of resources can be the situation when Guided Reading is a new initiative in a school. It can also be the case when Guided Reading is not a whole school initiative.

When children read in Guided Reading they are reading as independently as possible, that means they handle their own books. For the child 'looking over the shoulder' it would be distracting and replicates what happens in Round Robin reading, readers lose concentration. It is not the same, having someone else holding the book you are supposed to be reading. If resources are limited there are varied Guided Reading Material to resort to:

- Photocopied poems

- Photocopied articles from magazines, information from the newspapers, instructions e.g. how to complete an art project, how to work a washing machine

- Suitable comics

- Children's journals where there are multiple genres to read. For example, *Nelson Book Web* (Thompson Learning A/ia), *News* and *News Extra* (Horwitz Martin Education).

As quickly as possible, a selection of appropriate and varied good quality texts are purchased. Some schools I have visited have been in the situation where they lack resources and they began by ordering multiple copies of books for the lower grades (approximately 6 copies of each book) and gradually build on those by purchasing higher levels and novels (approximately 8 copies of each book). It is an expensive exercise and requires a lot of working together and planning. Ask book sellers to display the books at your school and you choose books generally suitable for your children.

Focal point: **Difficulties associated with levelling books**

Levelling of books is hard and mostly teachers rely on publisher levelling? It is a start. You may find though that you need to rely more on your experience and knowledge about your children and re-adjust the levels of certain books as you use them. You may find some books too hard at the level they are marked. If so change the level.

Also non-fiction books are given a much higher level because of the multi-layout of the texts, the formality of the language (not always like speech) and the unfamiliar technical vocabulary.

Current technologies allow children to move from the traditional hand-held-hard-copies to reading from ebook readers or tablet computers. Do not 'throw out' your hard copies but consider ordering and using **digital** guided reading books.

One suggestion: when you are sorting your books for Guided Reading, if possible, group them in **themes** to support topic work in the classroom (this especially applies to developing and early fluent texts).

Addendum

When to teach what!

Teaching Reading Strategies according to stages of Reading Development

Teachers respond to readers, the text, building on (day before) known

Emergent/beginner Readers - Levels 1-4

Directional movement Left-right/return sweep
1-1 matching finger/voice with the word ....pointing
Automatic response to 15 high frequency words (high frequency word centre) make analogies with known words,
Using picture cues, oral language structures, visual cue, **1st letter**
Questioning, 1st : *Does it make sense? Does it sound right?* 2nd : confirming, *Does it look right?*

Early Readers - Levels 5-8

Using two cueing systems – 1st, *Does it make sense?* and 2nd confirming , *Does it look right?*
Checking own reading using picture cues and 1-1 matching (eye pointing)
Re-reading to fix up own mistakes
When a child does **self correct, confirm that he has done the right thing** … "You self-corrected … that's what good readers do."
Building on known high frequency words – make analogies with known words, "You know 'went' this word has the same ending but begins with 's'
Looking at the initial letter and also **checking the ends of words**
Breaking words into syllables
If already read word or shown how to read a word – looks back to remind and help read the word again, "You read that word before, go back and re-read.

Becoming Fluent Readers - Levels 9-20

Beginning to use all 3 cues together when attempting a new word 1st , *Does it make sense?, Does it sound right?* Confirming, *Does it look right?* (especially 1st letter/final letter)
Questioning that encourages the reader to monitor closely … *You made a mistake, can you find it? You said ….. is that right?*
Frequently self-correcting – give children time to find their own mistakes. Wait until the end of the sentence or page before saying …. *Read that again and see if you can find your mistake.* Read the sentence to the child … *Does this sound right?*
Beginning to look at more print detail e.g. middle vowels, blends, compound words

Fluent Readers - Levels 21+

Nearly always using all cues, Meaning, Structure and Visual (all parts) to work out unknown words
Questioning … *How did you work that word out?*
Reads ahead

(from Reading Recovery handout)

Reading Programme ... what do you do?

Assessment:
Test Concepts of Print *(knowledge)*
Running Record (*reading behaviour*)
Letter/word knowledge
Keep a daily record
Keep a progress graph of the class (*moving up levels to approx. level 20*)
Assess comprehension responses to text (*e.g. oral, drawing, writing, projects*)

Reading:
Read Aloud (*Teacher reading*)
Individual (*e.g. pleasure, silent, conferencing with teacher, Book Clubs/discussion, literature, multi-texts (e.g. articles)*
Partner (*e.g. research*)
Shared/Guided/Reciprocal
-   Emphasis, instruction meaning (*e.g. book introductions - précis, story-line, predictions*)
-   Retell, summarizing, comprehension, exploratory talk
-   Focused language study, (*words, grammar, punctuation*)
Learning strategies to work on words/thinking strategies
Planning the teaching point (focus) *makes impact by extracting it from continuous print*
Balance support/new challenge
Use 3-steps to independence –
1. Model 'self-questions' and instruction *meaning,* (e.g. *What is the character doing?*); visual (e.g. *What does the word begin with? Visualize the setting*);
2. Prompt (e.g. *What would you do to solve that problem?*);
3. Shifting responsibility to child (e.g. *How did you work that out?*).
Audio stories with children reading along
Using computer (*e.g. kid pix + slide shows, CD Rom, excel, word 7, internet, office publisher, e-mail, internet, power point, interactive whiteboard, and the list keeps growing!*)
Grouping children at same developmental level
Levelled Texts (text match) – levels 1-20
Grouping children with same interests

Organize independent work when small group/individual teaching happens:
-   Behaviour rules set/displayed
-   Gradual introduction to activities
-   Pre-skilling use of new activities/behaviour
-   Use management task board or baskets with activities (baskets placed on desks)
-   Literacy learning to meet child's needs
-   Stimulating environment
-   Children consult management task board (*easy access*)
-   Equipment/activities stored in a specific area, kept in learning centres, and labelled
-   Quiet area kept for small group instruction. Guided reading material close at hand – (*each group, a box (or similar) containing levelled books for that day, daily record sheets, running record sheets*)

Chart this reminder!

THINKING about your reading

Follow this **thinking map**

PLOT

Main Parts of the story – beginning, middle, ending

What happened ………?

How did the story [end]?

What was the problem? What was the solution?

CHARACTERIZATION

Who were ………?

What did they do?

SETTING

Where was …………

NON FICTION

What is the title?

What do the contents say?

What does the topic sentence say?

What information follows the topic sentence?

Information about Interactive Writing

Interactive writing is a supportive method a teacher uses with new or unsure writers. During this teaching and learning situation ideas are nurtured and children are shown how language composes a story.

With teacher support the children jointly construct a piece of writing, sharing the same pen to construct text they would not be able to do alone. The children first think of an idea and each child has a turn writing on a large sheet of paper or white board, words or parts of words. Children learn to begin sentences with capitals, finish with full stops, directional behaviours, spacing and problem solving strategies for spelling words (e.g. hearing sounds in words).

A medium-sized alphabet board is displayed close to a medium-sized whiteboard children are able to write on. This enables them to make phoneme and grapheme connections, see the shape of the letter they want to produce.

Each child has a small whiteboard (or chalkboard) and marker (or chalk) and at times you ask them to practise on their personal boards, for example, writing 'I' on the left top side.

As soon as you see children beginning to write some words, Shared Writing may be sufficient only. The idea of Interactive Writing is to have a small group of about 6 uncertain writers only. They especially respond to the small group joint construction of texts.

(excerpt from, soon to be published manuscript *Let's Conference Reading and Writing*).

Information about a guide to encourage Independent Research

The authors, Rindi Baildon and Mark Baildon (2008), are the creators of the 3-point Research Resource guide **R**eadability, **T**rustworthiness, **U**sefulness (RTU) which assists students to become independent readers and researchers.

Explicit instruction of how to use the guide, for example, whether to read a particular text or move to another text, how to discover suitability themselves by being able to evaluate information sources.

Criteria for developing **R**eadability:	Criteria for **T**rustworthiness:	Criteria for **U**sefulness:
. Can I read and understand this on my own? . Is it a 'just right' read for me? . Can I understand most of the words and not lose meaning if I have to skip words? . Is the layout easy enough to follow?	. Can I find an author or a publisher's name? . Can I find at least one other source with the same information? . Have I found this same information in other books or websites . Is the information current? . Do I recognize the author or creator?	. Does this resource have what I am looking for? . Is this worthwhile, or am I wasting my time on this resource? . Does it follow my research plan, the questions I have asked which relate to the Big Question? . Do I need it? . Do I need to move to another resource?

(more information on *lizsimonliteracyconsultant.Blogspot.com* (2012 entry)

BLM 1: *(See Black line master 4 for blank copy)*
Guided Reading – Early Readers (levels 1-9)

Group *Recording Example*

Before reading:	*Knowing the story ... predicting (title, cover, text illustrations)*
During reading:	*Think about the story, listen to yourself read, modelling comprehension, 'fix-up' strategies*
After reading:	*Retell, after approx L.6 Partner retell. Discussion – pre-planned open ended questions, show a strategy on a word. Go to 'After Guided Reading practise a word' centre*

Date	L	Book title	Discussion focus / Word strategy	Comment
	A L L L E V E L 1 BOOKS 2 2 2 2 2 3 3 3 3		What is your favourite part? Why? *What happened first, last, middle?* *is* *the* *link* *in* *and* *me* *link* *be* *am* *look* *can* *on* *my* *link* *by*	**MP- (child's initials)** not looking at pictures for cues. *During Shared Reading demonstrate how pictures help to predict some words. During Guided Reading, carefully 'read' the pictures – text/picture match.* **LR- Not able to retell story** *I give more in depth book introduction (illustrations, predictions, relate to prior knowledge).* *Pre-practise new, unusual words.* *Read story in parts – stop ask "What happened at the beginning, then middle, then ending?"* *Remind to* **think about the story** *before child reads.* **CF- & VB-** Not looking at the first letter of a word. *During Shared Reading use a window device. Focus on the 1ˢᵗ letter of a word (check to see if CF knows what 'first' means').* Run Rec 3/5 **MP-** Looking at 1ˢᵗ letter fairly secure, now attention to endings.

BLM 2: *(See Black line master 5 for blank copy)*

Guided Reading – Developing Readers Group approx Level 10 +

Group   *Recording Example*

Before reading: *Knowing the story ... predicting (title, cover, text illustrations)*

During reading: *Think about the story, listen to yourself read, model comprehension strategies, 'fix-up' strategies mainly ask "How can you help yourself?" "What strategy did you use...?"*

After reading: *Partner retell, discussion – pre-planned open ended questions, quick word strategy*

Date	L	Book title	Discussion focus Word strategy	Comment
	10		**What was the problem?**	2/3 Run Rec **ST**- (child's initials) read fluently, comprehending at this level, using predicting, connecting strategies throughout reading, discussion.
	10		**What was the solution?**	
	10			
			What would you suggest as a solution?	**LE**- leaving out words that distort meaning. Give cut up sentence work.
	11			
	11			**BL**- reread to regain meaning.
			Compare the character's behaviour in this book to ...	Run. Rec **JT**- 5 errors, each time SC. Before reading remind to look carefully at words. Demonstrate 'come' 'came' with magnetic letters . Before reading remind to look at endings, inflections.
			Why do you think the author called the story ... What strategy are you using?	**VM**- 5-6 words couldn't read. Take back a level Use PM's to build up high frequency words. Independent Activities - word centre.
			Tell a favourite fact	**KA**- S/C when it didn't make sense.
			Look into the middle of the word	

BLM 3: *(See Black line master 6 for blank copy)*

Guided Reading – Guided Reading – Early FLUENT Readers

Group   *Recording Example*

Before reading: *Knowing the story ... predicting (title, cover, text illustrations)*
During reading: *Think about the story, listen to yourself read, use comprehension strategies*
After reading: Preparing responses, *pre-planned open ended questions, discussion*

Date	L	Book title	Discussion focus New vocabulary	Comment
			. main ideas . would you recommend this book to a friend. Why? . interpreting character's actions . language that creates moods . exploring the theme . comparing stories (differences/sameness) You ask 2 open-ended questions about ... New word 'exploration'	**NH-** liking the humorous stories in the series. Try to find more books in this series. **RE-** not listening to other children's comments. Re-skill class in group participation behaviour. **Group-** Lots of discussion about character's actions. Using comprehension strategies, knowing text/language structures, inferring, summarizing. Follow up with another book that describes a different character's actions. 6/6 assessed comprehension of **GL-** √ **AL-** had difficulty isolating the solution. More work on creating own solutions before they read author's solution.

BLM 4: *Guided Reading – Early Readers (levels 1-9)*

Group

Before reading: *Knowing the story ... predicting (title, cover, text illustrations)*	

During reading: *Think about the story, listen to yourself read, modelling comprehension, 'fix-up' strategies*

After reading: *Retell, after approx L.6 Partner retell. Discussion – pre-planned open ended questions, show a strategy on a word. Go to 'After Guided Reading practise a word' centre*

Date	L	Book title	Discussion focus Word strategy	Comment

Liz Simon *Truly Guided Reading, 2014*

BLM 5: *Guided Reading – Developing Readers Group* approx Level 10+

Group

Before reading: *Knowing the story ... predicting (title, cover, text illustrations)*
During reading: *Think about the story, listen to yourself read, model comprehension strategies, 'fix-up' strategies* mainly ask *"How can you help yourself?" "What strategy did you use...?"*
After reading: *Partner retell, discussion – pre-planned open ended questions, quick word Strategy*

Date	L	Book title	Discussion focus Word strategy	Comment

Liz Simon *Truly Guided Reading,* 2014

BLM 6: *Guided Reading – Guided Reading –* Early FLUENT Readers

Group

Before reading: *Knowing the story ... predicting (title, cover, text illustrations)*
During reading: *Think about the story, listen to yourself read, use comprehension strategies*
After reading: Preparing responses, *pre-planned open ended questions, discussion*

Date	L	Book title	Discussion focus New vocabulary	Comment

Story Mapping

Read _____ **with a buddy.**

Make a story map with pictures and some words to tell what happened in the story.

Title:

Where, when, who?	What?	What	Ending?

Liz Simon *Truly Guided Reading* 2014

BLM 8: *Generic comprehension sheet*

	Cause of problem	

Create your own headings

Title:

	Effect of problem:	

Liz Simon *Truly Guided Reading 2014*

BLM 9: *Generic comprehension sheet*

RECOUNTING THE STORY

Name: Date:

Title

Characters:
Beginning:
Middle:
Ending:

BLM 10: *Generic comprehension sheet*

RECOUNTING THE STORY

Name: Date:

Title

Characters:

Problem:

Solution in story:

Your solution:

BLM 11: *Generic comprehension sheet*

FORMING OPINIONS

Name _____

Name of the book ....

Author's name ....

I have chosen:

The character ....

The plot is ....

Good points	Bad points

Liz Simon *Truly Guided Reading* 2014

BLM 12: *Generic comprehension sheet*

NON-FICTION NOTES SHEET

Title: Name:

INTERESTING FACT

Main Points:

Something you would like to know:

Liz Simon *Truly Guided Reading* 2014

BLM 13: *3-tiered task cards*

Meaning

Character behaviour in [fairy tale] e.g. Goldilocks, 3 Step Sisters/ Step mother, the wolf.	Draw 3 pictures of the character's behaviour.	R
	Write an apology letter to [ ] for the behaviour of [ ].	B
	Write interview questions to ask the badly behaved character.	Y

Meaning

Single, dual, or triple entries in Literacy journal Group R complete R Group B complete R,B Group Y complete all	Record your favourite quote or event from your reading. Why was it favourite?	R
	Thoughts and feelings from the book you have just read.	B
	Interview a classmate about the reading.	Y

Text Structure

Focus: writing adventure stories	Write a problem and write a solution the CHARACTER experiences.	R
	Write the cause, problem and solution the CHARACTER experiences.	B
	Work with a partner. Draw a MONSTER. Cut it in ½ (vertical direction) and swap one half with your peer. ½, 1 partner, write a problem the monster has. ½, 1 partner, write how he solves his problem?	Y

Liz Simon *Truly Guided Reading* 2014

BLM 14

Text Structure

Focus: Recount a story	Write how the story began and ended.	R
	Write a recount of all the parts of the story – beginning, middle, ending.	B
	Change the beginning and ending of the story.	Y

Language Structure

Focus: dialogue	Draw two characters talking to each other. Draw bubbles coming out of their mouths. Write a question one character asks and an answer the other character gives.	R
	Write one character talking to another character. Use punctuation marks to show what they are saying.	B
	Write a short story with a horse talking to a girl or boy. Use punctuation marks. Make the story humorous.	Y

Words

Focus: Words that sound the same	Read 'What's the weather?' Write 'weather' 3 times. It means...	R
	Write the meaning of weather.	B
	Write a 4 lined poem about how to remember the 'weather' spelling pattern.	Y

Liz Simon *Truly Guided Reading* 2014

BLM 15: *Reciprocal Teaching/Reading*

Group Names:

Write in each box: (Read the title, headings and content pages before you predict)

Predicting:
Write one or two sentences that predict what the rest of text will be about.

Questioning:
Ask open-ended questions for discussion.

Clarifying:
Write any words, phrases or ideas that puzzled you.

Summarizing:
Write a summary sentence about the passage/text you read

Liz Simon *Truly Guided Reading 2014*

After discussion with your group write in your journal any new insights.

Literacy Response Journal

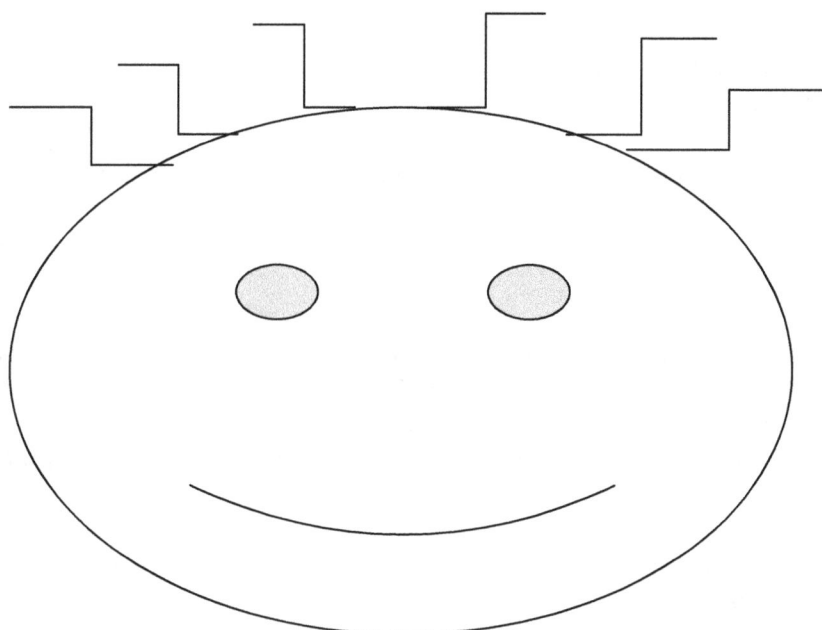

NAME:

Liz Simon *Truly Guided Reading* 2014

BIBLIOGRAPHY

Australian Curriculum and Reporting Authority (ACARA).
www.australiacurriculum.edu.au/English/Rationale) 2012.

Alphakids. 1998. Horwitz Publications. NSW 2065 Australia.

Alexander, Robin. 2010. *Speaking but not listening? Accountable talk in an unaccountable context.* Literacy v.44 no 3 p 106.

Baildon, M., & Baildon, R (2008). Guiding Independence: Developing a research tool to support student decision making in selecting online information sources. *The Reading Teacher,* 61(8), pages 636-647.

Clarke-Giles, Telene. Scott, Marjorie. 1996. *Rock and Roll Clyde.* First published Era Publications. Adelaide. South Australia.

Clay, Marie M. 2000 *Running Records for classroom teachers.* Heinemann. Portsmouth. NH.

Clay, Marie. 2007. *An Observation Survey of Early Literacy Achievement* (2nd ed), Heinemann, Portsmouth, NH

Concannon-Gibney,T & Murphy, B. 2010. *Reading practice in Irish primary classrooms: too simple a view of reading?* Literacy v.44 no.3. pages 124,125.

Croser, J and Kennedy, A. 1994. *Shut the door.* Era Publications, Adelaide. South Australia. 5025

Dalley-Trim, L. (2010). Popular culture in the classroom: A plethora of possibilities. In R. Henderson (Ed.), *Teaching Literacies in the middle years: Pedagogies and diversity (pp.81-110.* South Melbourne, Vic: Oxford University Press.

Fisher, Annie. 2008 Teaching *Comprehension and critical literacy: investigating guided reading in three primary classrooms.* The United Kingdom Literacy Association. Vol. 42. No 1. April. p.23.

Fleischman, Paul. 1997. *Seedfolks.* Joanna Colter Books. Harper Collins.

Fox, Mem. 2001. *Reading Magic. Why Reading Aloud to children will change their lives forever.* A Harvest Original. Harcourt Inc. New York. NY 10010.

Galdone, Paul. 1974. *The Three Billy Goats Gruff.* Windmill Press. Surrey. UK

Gibbon, Pauline. 1993. *Learning to learn in a second language.* Pearson Education Canada.

Hertzberg, Margery. 2009. *Reader's Theatre texts to improve fluency and comprehension.* e:lit – the Primary Teaching Association. N.S.W. 2204. Australia.

It's about Time. 2001. Orbit Collections. *Time.* Learning Media Limited. New Zealand.

Keene, Ellin and Zimmerman, Susan. 1997. *Mosaic of Thought*. Heinemann. Portsmouth. NH.

Literacy Collections 6 Middle {Primary. The emperor and the nightingale. Hans Christian Andersen. Rigby Heinemann. Victoria. A/1a.

Lock, Kath, Kely, Frances, Stafford, Katharine. 1995. *Deirdre of the Sorrows. Era Publications. South Australia.*

Nelson Book Web and Book Web Plus. Cengage Learning Australia and New Zealand. Victoria. Australia.

News and *News Extra*. Varied titles. (Horwitz Martin Education). St Leonards. NSW. Australia.

Nisbet Bain, R 2010. *Hans Christian Andersen, biography.* Nabu Press.

Nystrand et al (1997). *Opening Dialogue: Understanding the Dynamics of Language and Learning in the English Classroom*, New York: Teachers College Press pp. 30-74

Palinscar, A.S. and Brown, A.L. 1986. *Interactive teaching to promote independent learning from text.* The Reading Teacher, 39, 771-777

PM Alphabet Starters. 1995. First published by Nelson Price Milburn Ltd. Petone. New Zealand. Now Nelson Cengage Learning. South Melbourne, Victoria. Australia.

PM Library Starters One and Starters Two. 1995. First published by Nelson Price Milburn Ltd. Petone. New Zealand. Now Nelson Cengage Learning. South Melbourne, Victoria. Australia.

PM Story Books. 1994. First published by Nelson Price Milburn Ltd. Petone. New Zealand Now Nelson Cengage Learning. South Melbourne, Victoria. Australia..

Shanahan, C H (2008) *Reading and writing across multiple texts*. In K.A. Hinchman & H.K.

Sheridan-Thomas (Eds.) Best Practices in Adolescent Literacy Instruction (p.138). New York, US: The Guildford Press.

Simon, Liz. 2004. *Strategic Spelling* Every Writer's Tool. Heinemann, Portsmouth, NH USA. Now: www.amazon.com or www.barnesandnoble.com/w/strategic-spelling-liz-simon

Simon, Liz, 2010. *Thinkers and Performers Bringing Critical Thinking Alive*. HawkerBrownlow. Vic. Australia.

Simon, Liz, Blog, 2012: *How to assist your students become readers and researchers.* www.lizsimonliteracyconsultant.blogspot.com

Skidmore, David, Perez-Parent, Montserrat and Arnfield, Simon. UKLA Reading Literacy and Language c37.no.2. 2003. P. 52

Nelson Book Web. Thompson Learning A/ia. South Melbourne. Victoria. Australia.

Vygotsky, L. (1978). *Mind and Society*. Cambridge, MA: Harvard University Press.

www.ingramcontent.com/pod-product-compliance
Lightning Source LLC
Chambersburg PA
CBHW082033110426

42744CB00034B/1919